Mary Emmerling's
New Country
Collecting

Mary Emmerling's
New Country
Collecting

Text by Carol Sama Sheehan
Photographs by Joshua Greene

Design by Judy Schiern Hecker

Clarkson Potter/Publishers
New York

To my mother, Marthena Ellisor,
who will always be in my heart
To all the antiques dealers and private collectors
who have always been there for me

Also by Mary Emmerling
American Country
Collecting American Country
Mary Emmerling's American Country West
Mary Emmerling's American Country Cooking
Mary Emmerling's American Country Hearts
Mary Emmerling's American Country South
American Country Christmas
Mary Emmerling's American Country Classics
Mary Emmerling's American Country Gardens
Mary Emmerling's American Country Flags
Mary Emmerling's At Home in the Country
Mary Emmerling's American Country Christmas List Book
Mary Emmerling's American Country Cottages
Mary Emmerling's American Country Details

Published by Clarkson N. Potter, Inc., 201 East 50th Street, New York, New York 10022.
Member of the Crown Publishing Group.
Random House, Inc. New York, Toronto, London, Sydney, Auckland
CLARKSON N. POTTER, POTTER, and colophon are trademarks of
Clarkson N. Potter, Inc.
Manufactured in the United States
Library of Congress Cataloging-in-Publication Data
Emmerling, Mary Ellisor.
Mary Emmerling's new country collecting/by Mary Emmerling; text by
Carol Sama Sheehan; photographs by Joshua Greene.
1. Antiques business—United States.   2. Antique dealers—United States.
I. Sheehan, Carol Sama.   II. Greene, Joshua.   III. Title.
NK1133.28.E48   1996
745.1'092'273—dc20   95-30199
ISBN 0-517-58367-4
10 9 8 7 6 5 4 3 2 1
First Edition

Acknowledgments

The dealers and collectors in this book represent a cross section of the many people in the antiques trade who have been important to me over the years. Time and again, I have turned to them, not only for the things I love to collect, but for their knowledge of antiques and collectibles and for their friendship and support. We run into each other at antiques shows, in shops, and in one another's homes. Everyone is always on a quest. We may have different preferences in what we collect, buy, and sell, but we have a lot of things in common, too. The antiques business is exciting, unpredictable, ever-changing. There are affectionate and, occasionally, not so affectionate rivalries in the trade, but the business is so fascinating and rewarding that basically we are all in it together. I'd like to thank those friends "in the business" and the many others who helped with this book.

This has been a long and wonderful journey of antiquing and collecting—starting in Sugarbush, Vermont, as a young married couple growing from one apartment to another, upgrading and changing antiques and looks—but always collecting country.

The journey has taken me to many beautiful homes of antiques dealers and collectors from whom I have learned so much. Whether it was the history of an 18th-century American highboy (Morgan and Gerri MacWhinnie), or a simple idea of what to do with a collection of English matchstrikers (Carol Glasser), or how to display a collection of ironstone pitchers on a kitchen shelf (Peri Wolfman), or ideas from a way a dealer sets up a booth at an antiques show (Kate and Joel Kopp, America Hurrah) or from a field of dealers in the spring at Brimfield.

Everyone has been supportive. I can't thank each and every one of you personally, but this book is for all of you, to thank you from the bottom of my heart. From all the old friends to the new ones—a great group of friendships. To everyone who made this book happen:

The Benjamin Harrison Home, Mary and Marc Cooper, Rod Lich and Susan Parrett, Tasha and Jack Polizzi, Carol and Mark Glasser, Judith George and Adrian Cote, Jackie and Douglas Eichhorn, Susie and Rich Burmann, Richard Levey and Sigrid Christiansen, Robert Zollinhofer, Al and Marjorie Stauffer, Judy Conrad, Olga and Skipper Bowles, Barry and Dianne Cash, Carol Anthony, Ellen Windham, Paul and Sharon Mrozinski, Barbara Doherty, Joy Haley, Hannah and Art Stearns, Mark and Lisa McCormick.

I want to thank again and again Joshua Greene and Soffie Kage, who were always there for this book and the others we have done together. And to Michael Skott and Jeff McNamara, great friends and great photographers.

Always to my close friends (who I talk to mostly from airports), who are all true collectors—Lyn Hutchings, Beverly Jacomini, Patti Kenner, Buffy Birrittella, Irmgard St. John, Mibs Bird, Katrin Cargill, Peri Wolfman, Nancy Power, Ann Lawrence, Kathy Blue, Nancy Reynolds, Gloria List, Susan Victoria, Mark Dvorak, Peter Vitale, Trish Foley, Sandy Horvitz, and Chris Mead, who has been my friend for fifteen years.

A big thank you—always—to everyone at Clarkson Potter, especially to Lauren Shakely, who has always made this all happen, Diane Frieden, Judy Hecker, Howard Klein, Hilary Bass, Joan Denman, Jane Treuhaft, Maggie Hinders, Mark McCauslin, and Michelle Sidrane.

To Carol Sheehan, who knows be better than I do; to Melissa Crowley, who I can't do it all without; and to Janet Norales Bryant, again, for all of her excellent help on the directory.

To Jonathan and Samantha, for nothing would be worth it without them. Boy, am I lucky to have the best son and daughter in the world. To my brother, Terry, who collects nothing! And to Juanita Jones for her love and support for me, Jonathan, and Samantha.

Lastly, to my agents, Gayle Benderoff and Deborah Geltman—fifteen books later and they are still there for me—a big thank you!

Happy Collecting,

Mary Emmerling

Contents

Introduction   8

Collector's Choice

Learning to Grow a Collection   19

Bringing Character to a Room   28

Living with Native American
    History   37

The Comfort of the Past   46

A Cloister That Houses Tradition and
    Spirit   54

The Queen of Lean   62

Twin Cabins of Authenticity   70

Good, Better, Best!   76

Faith in the Original Design   84

A Comfortable and Venerable
    Homestead   91

Dealer's Choice

Using Fine Country Character and
    Style   105

An Eye for Choosing the Best   112

A Loyal Clientele   120

The Beauty of Original Details   126

A House Like No One Else's   134

Dealer's Country   142

Guided by Intuition   152

The Simple Honesty of the
    Ordinary   160

The Richness of the Unusual in
    Daily Life   167

Keeping the Faith   174

Guessing the Next Trend   182

Resource Guide   193

Index   207

Introduction

For the longest time I was under the impression that my fondness for collectors and dealers and my unbridled passion for collecting were simply a natural outgrowth of my early years in the magazine business. Working as a decorating editor in New  York City, I began exploring the world of antiques, and loved what I found there. In particular, I gravitated to rustic country furniture, folk art, American flags, baskets, redware and yellowware bowls, quilts, and many other things that represented to me one of America's most precious legacies, the heritage of the frontier.

Time revealed that perhaps some of my penchant for such things was inherited. I had always known there were very distinguished personages in my family tree. I am descended on my mother's side from the Harrisons, a family that came from England in 1632 to settle in Virginia. Two direct descendants of that family lived in the White House. William Henry Harrison, the ninth U.S. President (1841), was my great-great-great-great-grandfather. Benjamin Harrison, the twenty-third U.S. President (1889–1893), was my great-great-grandfather.

It was not until 1988 that I managed to visit the historic President Benjamin Harrison Home in Indianapolis, Indiana, for the first time. I knew the home existed even as a child, since it was part of our family history that my grandmother donated to the home furniture and keepsakes that had been handed down to her generation of the family from Benjamin Harrison's time. The antiques were used to help furnish the sixteen-room brick Italianate mansion that Benjamin had built for his wife, Caroline, in 1875. Ironically, the family's desire to help with the restoration project meant I would grow up without those antiques to enjoy!

In any case, when I finally visited the mansion, I was bowled over. In room after room, I discovered that the things the Harrison family of the late 19th century had collected were the very things I loved to bring into my

house more than a hundred years later. The library sported a Texas horn chair with leopard fabric—something I would snap up in a minute if I saw it on the antiques trail. The dining room had china with pansies on it, hand-painted by Caroline Harrison. As a longtime collector of paintings with that flower in them, I got goose bumps at that discovery, which made me feel a special connection with Caroline Harrison and with the past. In the restored kitchen stood that icon of Midwestern country furniture, the Hoosier cabinet, along with a Reliant woodstove, and, as a lighthearted, totally unpredictable element that made me smile, a gigantic birdcage.

Everything in that house, I came to understand, was something I love—flags, urns, velvet, log cabin quilts—all brought together in an updated fashion. It was not a typical dark and heavy Victorian interior. It was elegant, rather than overwrought,

and it seemed to convey wit, intelligence, and good humor.

I was also overwhelmed by the sheer history in the place. Every piece had been carefully researched and documented, and since virtually all of the pieces had been in my own family, that first visit became a kind of journey into my own past. It allowed me to appreciate my legacy in a personal way. I had understood the Harrisons in an intellectual way. Now it hit me that they truly were part of my family, in a binding emotional way, and I was part of theirs.

All this made me reflect that it was not mere coincidence that my "trademark" affection for hauling out the American flag, in sizes great and small, reflected one of President Benjamin Harrison's official acts in office—ordering the flag flown over all public buildings! I had not known that fact before my visit to Indianapolis.

Another unofficial act of his also echoes my own love of holiday traditions—he was the first President to bring a Christmas tree into the White House in December.

My visit to the

Harrison Home put me in touch with my roots as a collector as nothing before had ever done.

I have been a collector all my life. When I had shops in New York and in the Hamptons, out on Long Island, I wore a dealer's hat. Even today, working on decorating projects for my clients, I assume the role of dealer to obtain the furniture and accessories my clients desire. So I feel I am familiar with the challenges and the satisfactions to be found in both fields.

Although sometimes the lines blur, there are obvious distinctions between a collector and a dealer. A collector is motivated solely by a love for the thing. As Thatcher Freund observes in his book *Objects of Desire,* "All collectors place themselves into the things they buy." A dealer may love the thing as much, but can't afford not to sell it.

Frequently, collectors are more knowledgeable about the things they collect than dealers are, simply because they often have spent a lifetime focusing on their specific passion. In the course of

many hours of reading, tireless travel, and consultation with experts (some of whom may in fact be dealers), collectors become scholars of their "objects of desire."

As the collectors in this book will attest, collecting is a lifetime obsession. Most of them got started when they were children, without realizing it. Drawn to the beauty, charm, or novelty of something, they found pleasure in being able to own the thing, and variations on the thing, and before long they had their first collection on their hands. As collectors mature, their innate collecting abilities sharpen and their knowledge of the things they collect deepens. Good collections grow in quality as well as in size, as their creators "trade up." True collectors instinctively gather favorite objects that tend to be closely related in theme, usage, or style.

While some collectors are content to enjoy their cherished objects for their intrinsic qualities, others are sensitive to the stories the objects tell of their time and place. Still others are lucky enough to

have both, responding to the artistry in a collection of ancient Navajo weavings, for example, while at the same time becoming immersed in the history of the people who produced it. Mint-condition antiques are the exclusive (and expensive) purview of some collectors. Others are taken by things that bear the imprint of long usage. "All objects reveal usage by the way in which their color, texture, or shape is altered by time," observes Timothy Trent Blade in *Antiques Collecting*. "A colonial silver teaspoon will be covered with minute scratches which alter its reflective qualities; its bowl may be worn flat on its left side from repeated scooping by generations of right-handed owners."

Although it's hard to know what turns a collector into a dealer, one of my friends epitomizes what I feel is the dealer's characteristic independent and entrepre-

neurial spirit. As a girl, she was parliamentarian of her grammar school shell club. In the Girl Scouts, she collected fungi, then Indian nickels. Dolls, buttons, and purses soon followed. Later, in art school, she combed the flea markets for vintage clothes and worked part-time for a dealer who specialized in old Hollywood wardrobes. The dealer paid her in clothes, including a dress worn by Jean Harlow and a coat worn by Joan Crawford. When she left school, she sold the clothes to finance a trip to Europe. In Europe, she bought jewelry made by a nomadic Afghanistani tribe, which she sold for profit on her return. Next, saving her tip money from a restaurant job, she invested $3,000 in Native American pieces, and soon disposed of them for another handsome profit. All of this before she was twenty-one!

Dealers in antiques and collectibles come in many forms, from the "Treasure Chest" general-line variety on Main Street, U.S.A., where genuine antiques mingle amiably with secondhand furniture, gifts, and dubious collectibles, to

the high-end family-name firms found along Fifth and Madison Avenues in Manhattan, where the very best American and English antiques may be seen. Many dealers, including some featured in this book, do not have shops, but sell directly from their homes or in the temporary exhibits called antiques shows.

"Living with your inventory can pose some temporary inconveniences," notes dealer Susie Burmann. Everything in her house is for sale, so, she says philosophically, "sometimes we have a kitchen table, sometimes we don't."

Many dealers sell their wares exclusively through antiques shows, thus avoiding the expense of maintaining a retail outlet or the inconvenience of admitting strangers to their living quarters. Shows generate their fair share of browsers, but there are also many knowledgeable collectors in

attendance, prepared to put cash on the barrel if they see the right thing. "Shows are a great place to learn about the marketplace," observes dealer Rod Lich. "You see the trends

and price points. There might be a thousand qualified customers passing through your booth in a single weekend. In a store, it would take weeks and weeks to receive so many."

Most experienced dealers specialize in antiques of certain period, such as pre–Civil War American furnishings, or distinct styles, such as country primitive, or categories of goods, such as Chinese porcelain or old silver. For the customer, the virtue in doing business with specialists is that the antiques they carry are likely to represent the cream of the crop.

I have found that good dealers are great educators. The have broadened my appreciation and knowledge of antiques, helping me develop as a collector, and they have given me lots of new ideas for decorating with style. Gloria List, for example, introduced me to the religious art of Mexico and the Southwest, showing me how carved and painted images that once graced altars can make a similar impact on a rustic table in a city apartment.

Dealers have an eye for things of value and importance. A good dealer can breeze through a flea market covering many acres in no time, sizing up the offerings quickly, not wasting time on junk, and should the genuine article appear, making the deal with lightning-speed. Having seen literally thousands of country chairs, say, or weathervanes, the dealer has the background and experience to be so decisive.

A common passion unites the dealers and collectors in this book. All of them love their antiques and collectibles. They have to have them. They refuse to accept substitutes. The dealers have the intensity of the collectors, so much so that they are reluctant to part with the special object if the would-be buyer fails to demonstrate the same appreciation.

Dealers and collectors equally enjoy the adventure of the hunt. Even on a focused search for a specific piece, most will not hesitate to pounce on an unrelated treasure if it is a bargain. The lure of objects often draws the hunter far afield. There is as much thrill in the looking as in the finding, and the next day, it starts all over again.

The houses of dealers and collectors are unique showcases, full of rarities, yet warm and inviting—homes, not museums. Yet, because of the things that are in it, each house stands out as a distinct expression of one person's vision, and it is often museum-quality. Many people accumulate things, but the people featured in this book collect, not accumulate, and they collect with purpose, focus, direction, and passion. I hope their homes and collections will serve as an inspiration to others.

Collector's Choice

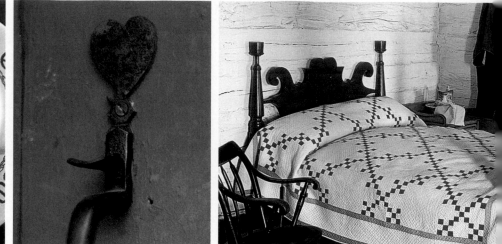

Israel Sack, Inc., one of the country's most respected dealers in early American furniture, bought a secretary desk at auction for $6,750 in 1950. Recently, the firm was offered more than $1 million for the same piece.

That, in a nutshell, is the story of American antiques since the midcentury mark. The surge in general interest, appreciation, and value has been astonishing, and the country's leading museums have organized departments and developed exhibitions to document and honor our decorative arts traditions, which no longer hold inferior status next to English and European styles.

Today, early American fine furniture is held in such high esteem that most of it is found in museums or the homes of very wealthy connoisseurs. There is little left on the market from before 1830, the era preceding the Industrial Revolution, and none of it at bargain prices. But collectors are intrepid and resilient folk. When one market loses interest or appeal, they find another.

"I noticed that the American antiques I was collecting skyrocketed in price after the Bicentennial in 1976," observes one collector. "That's when I started pursuing Mexican folk art—when masks could be obtained for $15—and that led me to the American Southwest and, eventually, to Spanish antiques."

 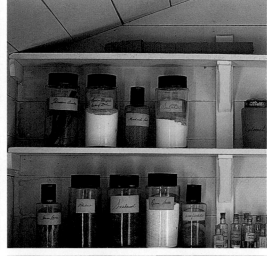

Other collectors have discovered that "perfect" things no longer interest them. "The older I get, the more interested I am in the sociology of the thing," admits another. "Now, if a beautiful piece of old china has a chip, it doesn't even bother me. I esteem it more because it's something that's had a life—it's been used."

In the eyes of the U.S. Customs Service, anything created more than a hundred years ago is not subject to duty upon entering this country. Among collectors, that has been the traditional method for defining what constitutes an antique. In reality, virtually any piece of Americana dating from before 1945 now enjoys the status of antique, because it is considered desirable both by collectors and dealers.

At first, traditionalists snubbed the more newly made "collectibles," but today these wares enjoy a peaceful coexistence because of the wide range of goods. When a 1969 Mattel Hot Wheels toy van sold for $4,025 at auction recently, Israel Sack might well have shuddered, but it marked the coming of age of the collectibles market.

Many of the collectors in this book, while amassing wonderful arrays of "serious" antique furnishings, also found time to put together smaller collections of things of less value but no less interest.

The 1770s New England banister-back armchair with heart cut-out and original paint is an auction prize. "I bought it years ago for $750," says Judy Conrad of her all-time favorite find. OPPOSITE: In the entryway of the 1840s house, a mural in the style of an early Maine artist, Rufus Porter, depicts sailing life on the Portage Lakes.

Learning to
Grow a Collection

THE RELATIONSHIP FORGED between collector and dealer is a special one. It is the collector's obsession that feeds the dealer's passion. When Judy Conrad walked in the late Dottie Williams's Saginaw, Michigan, antiques shop some twenty-five years ago, it was the beginning of a friendship that would spawn a lifetime of collecting. "This was the first time I had ever been in an antiques store, and when I walked into Dottie's shop, I wanted to move right in," Judy recalls. "That's when I thought to myself, If I feel this strongly about these things, I ought to have them in my house. That's the moment I became a collector."

At the time, Judy was a young wife and mother, running a busy household on a tight budget. "We were renting a house with a mantel over the fireplace," she recalls. "I noticed how Dottie had arranged a collection of old pewter on the shop's mantelpiece and I thought, Wouldn't that look nice in our house!" But she also knew that the financing for such

A kitchen equipped with period cooking implements and outfitted with furniture of the era reflects a collector's desire for fitting in furniture as it might have looked in a house of the 1840s. The mantel shows off old redware crock canisters. The two-drawer table with scrubbed lift top has a Hepplewhite base, with original red paint.

a purchase would have to come out of the family's grocery budget. "It would have taken a month's worth of groceries to bring a significant amount of the pewter home, and a diet of peanut butter and jelly for the family."

A dealer's willingness to strike flexible arrangements with clients sometimes builds long-term loyalty and rewards. "Dottie said, 'Go ahead, take the pewter home and enjoy it,'" explains Judy. "She let me put a little bit down and pay as I could." Over time, Dottie saw Judy's collection grow from those few pieces of pewter to a house full of early- and mid-18th-century antiques distinguished by their remarkable original color.

Along the way, Dottie tutored Judy in the art of antiques. "She was very generous with her knowledge of furniture and gave me some great advice," such as: "If you can obtain an antique for the same price as an equivalent new piece of furniture, buy the antique." Or, "If there is even the slightest nagging doubt or question about an antique you are considering buying, walk away from it."

Judy's passion for 18th-century furnishings informs every room of the Conrads' 1841 Pennsylvania-style cut-stone house in Clinton, Ohio, from the 1790 Chippendale-style cupboard with original gray-blue paint in the kitchen, to the early-18th-century Connecticut River Valley gateleg table that stands in the parlor against a bittersweet-colored, hand-stenciled wall. She and her husband, Dennis, stenciled the fleur-de-lis designs in mustard and

ABOVE LEFT: From a cornerstone found in the yard, the Conrads were able to date their house from 1841. TOP: The brilliant color of Chinese lantern brightens a dark background. ABOVE: Paint-decorated early American turned wooden bowls grew into a collection from one bought as a centerpiece. A collection of plates is stored in an 18th-century red-painted open cupboard built expressly to hold pewter. OPPOSITE: Skeins of wool colored with natural dyes hang from a peg rack underneath a shelf of redware jugs and an attractive drying basket.

green, after an authentic period design they had traced to an inn in Pennsylvania. "I wanted everything to look like it fit in," Judy says.

The Conrads have observed that antiques often stand out against the white walls found in new houses, eliciting the comment of visitors. "But I like them best in old houses," says Judy. "The antiques blend in and look like they belong."

As a collector, Judy is less sensitive to market fluctuations than a dealer must be. "Stoneware prices might be up and basket prices down, but livability is more important to me than cost," Judy explains. "For me the first question I ask of an antique is 'Will I enjoy living with it?'" Not that she is unmindful of market value. As a "security-minded Taurus," she views her antiques as money in the bank. "They're really a sound investment," she notes. "Ever since I first started collecting, I learned that I could always sell what I bought and get what I paid for it—if not more."

Had I bought new furniture, instead of antiques, it would just be considered 'used,' and if I tried to sell it today, it would be at a significant loss."

For Judy Conrad, her collection is an investment that brings far more pleasure than numbers on paper. As a collector educated by a dealer she has both the courage to sell when necessary and the sense to keep what "fits in."

ABOVE: A simple wood shelf holds beloved antiques, including a growing collection of railroad toys.
BELOW: Crewelwork curtains hang in a room where Dennis Conrad's love of the sea is represented by the relief-carved and painted clipper ship, early 19th century, and three lightship baskets from Nantucket. The hanging shelves were made in Ohio in the 1840s.
OPPOSITE: After decades of collecting, the owner can always make room for one more candlestand, especially if it is a rare 1780s snakefoot-style piece. The 18th-century New England ladderback chair is valued for its original paint with mustard trim. A local artist created the floor cloth with diamond pattern and marbleizing.

found Collections

The astute amateur naturalist can assemble an unexpected collection of beautiful objects found in nature. A

walk through a park, along a shore, or in the woods near one's house can yield as interesting an array of specimens as a trip to some exotic Patagonia.

The Victorian English made collecting exotica an art in the 19th century, bringing back to their parlors mementos from the far-flung corners of their empire. Specimen cases became a fixture in these homes, functioning as the entertainment center of the day, a perpetual source of wonder and knowledge about the newly unfolding mysteries of the natural world.

Without turning a room into a museum or mausoleum, as some eccentric and zealous collectors are inclined to do, people who appreciate nature can forage in many easily accessible places to successfully embellish a niche, wall, or tabletop in their home.

AT THE SEASHORE. Shells, sea glass, starfish, driftwood, and other items that the tide brings in offer an infinite variety of decorating ideas. A giant nautilus shell is pretty in itself, or, when arranged with other materials in an elegant urn, makes a mantel centerpiece. Fill an antique platter with sea glass and let light show it off. Look for scraps of wood that the sea has shaped into interesting forms, then recycle them as abstract sculpture on a porch or in the garden.

IN THE WOODS. Victorians were dedicated naturalists, scrupulously making "real" botanical prints out of speci-

mens found in a forest or home garden. Today, fern fronds, wildflowers, and fall maple foliage can be pressed and arranged in collages, then framed, to add a touch of natural beauty to a bare wall.

Fill a pretty vase or a wicker creel with a fistful of colorful grouse, pheasant, and wild turkey feathers found along a trail. For a more ambitious undertaking, look for abandoned birds' nests in autumn, after leaves have fallen. A half-dozen nests, from the simple abode of the robin to the complex weaver's dwelling, can make a stunning visual statement when carefully arranged in the house. A twiggy branch full of crooks or an old wire rack might be suitable for mounting the nests for display. Or collect old birdcages, furnish them with the nests, and decorate with a "found" collection of eggs of different sizes, shapes, and hues.

IN THE WILD. Cowhands have long scavenged the range for natural artifacts, from cow skulls to shed antlers, which become decoration for ranch houses. Skulls might simply be leaned against the side of a doorway, or hung over a mantel like a trophy. Antlers become chandeliers, candleholders, and even furniture.

You don't have to be a wrangler to keep your eye out for bleached bones, horseshoes, bottle dumps, old tools, and other remnants of farm, range, and campsite. Collectors who go river rafting or backpacking often come back from the wilderness with token reminders of their adventures, which they then incorporate into their homes. For stay-at-homers, there are always flea markets and other resources for bagging trophies of the wild.

Bringing Character to a Room

DON'T BUY ANYTHING larger than your suitcase." That is the rule that governs the collecting habits of Houston, Texas, interior designer Carol Glasser when she is traveling. The rule may sound restrictive, but, it turns out, a lot can fit in Carol's suitcase. Over the years, she has assembled collections of small silver objects, wicker-wrapped bottles, sturdy baskets, and blue-and-white Staffordshire dishes. In addition, she has found room to pack such finds as small paintings and engravings, gilded candlesticks, tapestries, and needlepoint textiles (to cover ottomans and pillows).

"Part of me craves a sparse, spare look," she admits, "and the other part of me needs to bring home a little treasure from every shopping trip. Guess which part of me usually wins!"

Her discoveries range from the whimsical, such as the antique French birdcage in her bedroom, to the ineffable, such as the first series of engravings ever made from

Carol Glasser uses everything from French urns to paisley shawls to infuse rooms with comfort and romance. OPPOSITE: An imposing array of antique blue-and-white Staffordshire china and black-lettered creamware shows the collector's eye and her love for beautiful, functional objects.

A casual chair and ottoman combine with an antique English writing table and chair to add utility and grace to the master bedroom. Wicker baskets and trays keep periodicals and paperwork organized, and the antique French birdcage introduces some whimsy to the room.

ABOVE: Tole trays with hand-decorated surfaces are favorites of the owner. She uses them to anchor small collectibles such as silver dressing table accessories or to add interest on their own. RIGHT: Old paisleys, tapestries, and a faded Oushak rug give the library an inviting, timeworn appearance. OPPOSITE: Tricks for effectively arranging collections include organizing objects by size, from the most dominant, or tallest, to the smallest, and varying textures, such as tole, silver, wood, and tin, within one area.

original Raphael paintings, which occupy the place of honor over her bed.

From her first trip to England while still in college, travel has strongly influenced Carol's eclectic style. Her house, which she shares with her husband, Mark, radiates a taste for romantic European cultures and classic styles. "I have as many French as English things," she notes, "as many Dutch as Italian pieces. I love drawing on different cultures and making objects work together."

Carol also loves to make the objects work, period. The first antique she ever bought was a pewter charger, which she has since used as a serving platter, a bin to hold family snapshots, and as a wall and shelf decoration. When she takes down a jug of milk-white creamware, originally gleaned on one of her trips through the English countryside, it might be used as a vase for flowers or a pitcher for iced tea or lemonade. Other assorted vessels have doubled as potpourri platters, fruit bowls, and bulb pots. Nothing she owns is allowed to collect dust.

Carol can always find room for one more charming piece. "Antiques are like old friends to me. If the piece is good, it keeps giving back to you." She'll move them around from room to room and dress up an old sofa or chair with a new slipcover or a paisley shawl, drawn from her collection of vintage textiles.

"Antiques are what bring character to a room," she believes, but as passionate as she is about antiques, Carol is equally passionate about comfort. "Who wants to live in a house that feels like a museum?" she asks. Her advice to clients is always the same—use collections to enhance the house and give it atmosphere. "The best houses, after all," says Carol, "are records of a lifetime."

Smalls—little things that mean a lot

The indomitable turn-of-the-century novelist and decorating guru Edith Wharton went to great lengths to justify a  place in the American home for the things other cultures called bric-a-brac, bibelots, or objets d'art.

"Decorators know how much the simplicity and dignity of a good room are diminished by crowding it with useless trifles," she and Ogden Codman, Jr., wrote in their classic *The Decoration of Houses*. Wharton was vehemently opposed to the indiscriminate amassing of "ornaments" or "commercial knickknacks," but she believed just as strongly that "good objects of art give to a room its crowning distinction."

In today's eclectic interiors, there is always room for at least one collection of diminutive objects, often referred to as "smalls" by antiques dealers and collectors—because the objects collected are usually small enough to carry out of the shop.

In her extensive travels, interior designer Ellen Windham is always on the lookout for something special that she can bring back to the house, so long as it is portable. In this way, over the years, she has assembled an elegant collection of petite picture frames in pewter, silver, and tin.

Other appealing focal points for a collector of smalls: coin silver, tiny animal paintings, porcelain figures, footed bowls, alabaster fruit, Shaker boxes, children's watering cans, old pincushions, hearts, Victorian calling card boxes, mantel clocks, miniature chairs, antique writing implements . . . and anything else, really.

Grouped together, smalls acquire a weight, importance, visual interest, and narrative power they could not possibly attain on their own. It takes more than a few pieces to constitute a recognizable grouping of smalls, but it may not take as many as you think. It all depends on the size of the object. As beautiful as they may be, five vintage fountain pens may get lost no matter where you exhibit them, but fifty pens won't go unnoticed. A collection of only a dozen blue-and-white Chinese porcelain vases, however, can serve as focal point in a room, atop a painted chest of drawers. Tabletops, hanging shelves, mantelpieces, and other niches in the house become theatrical backdrops for the play of form, color, and texture that the collections project. And they are small enough to move to new locations with ease as time and desire dictates.

Pick your smalls well. Classic rather than quaint or trivial should be the guiding principle. Too often, a collection begun on impulse can get out of hand. A friend happened to bring a few figures of frogs into her garden. Before long, thanks to the generosity of well-meaning friends, her house and garden were overrun with amphibians in concrete, terra-cotta, marble, porcelain, and a dozen other materials. "I was frogged out," the friend confessed.

On the other hand, the same friend became quite enamored of a collection of botanical pen-and-ink studies that came together for her almost unwittingly as she pursued her natural curiosity about horticulture. When smalls have relevance for the collector, they are more likely to hold perennial interest.

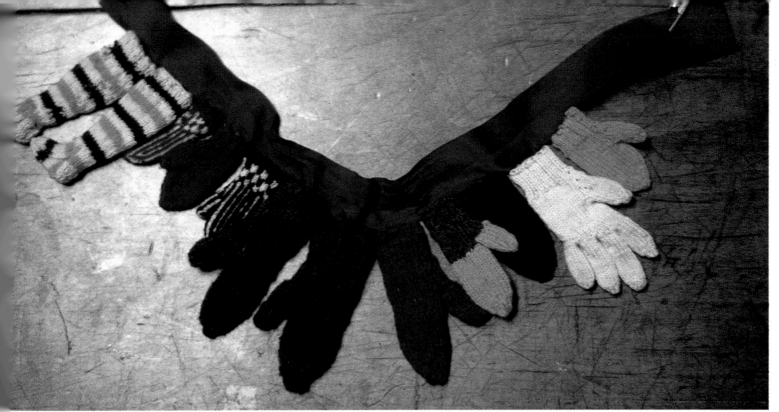

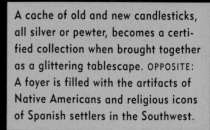

A cache of old and new candlesticks, all silver or pewter, becomes a certified collection when brought together as a glittering tablescape. OPPOSITE: A foyer is filled with the artifacts of Native Americans and religious icons of Spanish settlers in the Southwest.

Living with Native American History

OR DIANNE CASH, COLLECTING began as an innocent childhood pastime. She bought her first turquoise ring when she was seven, using her birthday money. Beachcombing along the Texas Gulf Coast, she gathered up whatever she came across. "Seashells were probably my first collection," she recalls. But it was the accumulated effect of many family vacations in the West, primarily in New Mexico, that shaped Dianne's present collecting focus. "I grew up with a great affection for the Native American culture," she says, and an appreciation for its colorful past. "History is really what I collect," and it informs every surface of her Spanish Colonial adobe dwelling in Santa Fe, New Mexico.

After twenty-five years of "adding a little piece here, a little piece there," her collection of Native American crafts has expanded to reflect the multi-ethnic community of the region, including New Mexican and Spanish religious artifacts, Mexican folk art, Spanish furniture, Western

The Cash home combines both sides of the Southwest style: rustic and refined. ABOVE: In the guest house, furniture in the tradition of the Great Camp was crafted by Dallas artisan Doug Marsden out of native crepe myrtle boughs. ABOVE RIGHT: A collection of Mexican *santos* (saints), missing their customary robes, takes on a theatrical presence when thoughtfully arranged. OPPOSITE: *Milagros* (tiny religious tin figures used to beseech favors or give thanks), sacred hearts, foreign coins from travels, and other trinkets put a distinctive face on a heavy wooden door.

relics, and even Moroccan antiques. "I never started out to develop a quote-unquote collection of any one thing," says Dianne. "But I do have a vision as I go about making the things in a collection work together."

Dianne's style is to put herself in the context of a specific place and time in history. "I like to imagine what it must have been like to live in a certain period—what people lived with, what they wore, how they went about daily life," she explains. For example, the eclectic English interiors of her Dallas home, rich in mahogany and teak, were inspired by "imagining an Englishman who had moved to Dallas after being stationed in India and China for so long that he brought all his furnishings with him when he moved."

Her cinema verité approach to decorating can be seen in the New Mexico house, which is old Santa Fe to the core—many people don't realize the city dates back more than three centuries. "I imagined the kinds of things a Spaniard would bring with him from his homeland in the 1700s—ornate Spanish, Italian, and English furnishings that would begin to feel at

RIGHT: Very old pots from Morocco proudly sport their vibrant colors and scars of daily use. BELOW: An old player piano, staple of the Victorian parlor, still cranks out music in a den where scores of moccasins and a Third Phase Chief's blanket enliven the walls. OPPOSITE: A local tinsmith transformed the mundane, covering both refrigerator and kitchen cabinets with pierced decorated tin.

home in the New World as Native American items worked their way into daily use and Westernized the household," she explains.

Dianne's husband, Barry, fosters role-playing with his own collection of hats, originally mostly Western and Indian headwear, now expanded by the generosity of friends to include hats from all over the world. "For a dinner party, we might have each guest pick out a hat to wear for the evening," says Dianne, "and enact the character who might have worn the hat."

Although she strives for historical authenticity in her collections, Dianne does not rope off her rooms in velvet. The dining room is mostly Spanish, with altar pieces adding their imposing presence. The kitchen is adorned with Mexican folk art figures. The bedrooms of her children are Western, and the den is a mix of Indian and Spanish—with Moroccan doors a very different style entryway. In every room, the furnishings and objects are treated like ordinary household items, for everyone to use and enjoy.

Dianne's most recent enthusiasm, for religious icons and artifacts, has led to the acquisition of some rarities, such as the 16th-century Spanish vestment that she uses as a table runner. "But I'm not trying to find the best of specimens, necessarily. The most interesting things aren't always the most expensive. I've found pleasing things of great value or little value" in flea markets or fine arts galleries.

"I'm not proud," she laughs. "If I like it, I'll take it wherever I can find it!"

LEFT: The ritual function of Native American clothing is celebrated in a wall display of garments from various tribes, including a Sioux wedding dress, a Crow warrior shirt and leggings, an Apache puberty dress, and pink Cheyenne leggings. Beaded birds decorate the Paiute infant cradle board. RIGHT: Lace panels found in England, originally intended to dress windows, show their versatility as bed hangings in a guest room. BELOW: A Western theme in the boys' room is carried out in new cowboy-boot fabric, a buffalo-hide Indian painting, and old rustic beds from Saltillo, Mexico.

native crafts of the Southwest

More than thirty tribes of Native Americans in Arizona and New Mexico continue to work in crafts traditions that began centuries ago, some before the arrival of  the Europeans, others inspired by materials the Europeans brought with them. Descendants of the early Spanish settlers and other groups also contribute to the rich artistic legacy of the region.

POTTERY is still made by Native Americans as it was 1,600 years ago, using local clays, skilled handwork in place of a potter's wheel, and primitive kilns. There are dozens of unique styles, ranging from simple storage vessels to elegant bowls and jars to humorous animal figures.

KACHINA DOLLS are the painted and carved wood figures made to represent the deities of the Hopi, Zuni, and other tribes. The male dancers who impersonate the deities in religious ceremonies give them to children in the pueblo where they perform. There are some 200 kachinas, each representing the spirit of some creature, place, or thing, with names like Owl, Mudhead, Black Ogre, Early Morning, and Spotted Corn.

BASKETS. Although many tribes make baskets, the Papagos of southern Arizona are the most productive and, some say, among the most creative. A typical Papago basket is made of a coil of bear grass sewn with bleached yucca and the black outer covering of the seed pod of devil's claw. Designs are simple patterns, animals, or people. Basket prices are determined by the fineness of the weave, the amount of stitching, the evenness of the shape, and the intricacy of the design.

NAVAJO RUGS. The Navajo, the largest tribe in the United States, learned weaving from the Pueblo Indians, using wool they obtained from the sheep Spanish settlers brought over. In the 18th and 19th centuries, tribal craftswomen produced finely woven blankets, then, with the introduction of machine-made fabric, shifted their energies to heavier pieces suitable for floor coverings, with large geometric designs with borders. One of the most famous, Chief's Pattern, with diamonds on a field of bold stripes, originally was the pattern used in blankets worn by Navajo men. Beginning in the 1930s, a wide range of vegetable dyes were used to add beautiful natural colors to the rugs.

CHIMAYO WEAVINGS were made in the Spanish-American village of Chimayo in northern New Mexico's Rio Grande valley. Early Chimayo weavings are considered to be as fine as that turned out by the best weavers of Mexico at Saltillo. Originally made on foot-operated looms with flying shuttles, Chimayo serapes were highly valued for their intricate patterns of concentric diamonds and a rich harmony of colors, frequently combinations of reds, yellows, and tans.

TRADE BLANKETS, machine-woven wool blankets with dazzling patterns and colors inspired by Native American basketry, ceramics, and textiles, were sold by trading posts in great numbers from the 1880s to about 1930. They were made by American mills, such as Pendleton and Oregon City, who advertised that to own such a blanket "was to own a piece of the vanishing romance of the American West."

The Comfort of the Past

AT FIRST GLANCE, there seem to be few modern conveniences at Cabin Creek Farm, the home of Hannah and Art Stearns in the heart of tobacco country, not far from Louisville, Kentucky, "remote from the rest of this bust world," as Hannah says. But look more closely. The clothes washer is hidden behind a cupboard. The dryer's out on the porch. The modern stove has an old cutting board on top of the burners. The TV is in the bedroom, atop a painted farm table.

The Stearnses much prefer old comforts to modern ones, a predilection formed by their common New England heritage. The compound on their forty-acre farm in Kentucky consists of a poplar log cabin built in 1863, which serves as the couple's living quarters, another cabin of equal vintage, used as Hannah's antiques shop and showroom, and a tin-roofed workshop that looks a hundred years old, built by Art. Here, they

Vintage cookie cutters, displayed in an old dough bowl in the kitchen, are as useful for making baked goods today as they were when new. OPPOSITE: Hannah and Art Stearns transformed an ordinary yellow kitchen cupboard into a primitive work of art, using one of the many paint-finishing techniques they have perfected.

fashion "aged" hand-painted signs with nostalgic sentiments such as "Homespun," "Hollyhocks," and "Never Enough Thyme," and paint new pantry boxes, peg racks, firkins, bowls, and baskets to resemble the utilitarian objects of old.

Decorating with her collections, Hannah has transformed the old cabin into a cozy, compact residence. The keeping room's creek-stone fireplace found in a local shop and bought before the cabin was built, is framed with an 1840s mantel. Mismatched chairs—"orphans," says Hannah—and a weathered farm table furnish the dining room. Art crafted their beds from sassafras gathered in the surrounding woods. The same irregular, rustic charm defines their herb and flower gardens, which Art fenced off with rough-sawn pickets of varying heights and widths as a study in country nonconformity.

Wherever they have lived, Hannah has run a shop. "I've always collected and sold things," she says, prowling junk shops, flea markets, consignment stores, and tag sales in pursuit of elusive treasures, but staying away from auctions, "because everything is already there, and I like the fun of the hunt."

As many collectors will attest, sometimes an old thing buys you even before you buy it. Years ago, when Hannah was just getting started collecting her utilitarian objects, she came upon a basket that intrigued her. "The asking price was $20, which seemed like a lot of money to me back then," she recalls. "I hesitated before buying it because of a piece of tape on the handle. I thought perhaps the tape was there to conceal a flaw. But when I peeled it off, I saw the initials *E.M.* carved into it—the same initials as mother's, who had recently passed away. I knew I had to have it."

ABOVE: An early amateur furnituremaker's version of a slant-top desk serves as an artist's catch-all. Rulers are kept in a hollowed-out log. LEFT: A checkers set, with all pieces intact, rests beside an early ladderback chair with hide seat and original blue paint. OPPOSITE: In a household that looks devoid of modern technology, a red lift-top desk hung on the wall cleverly conceals an answering machine and telephone. A locally found cupboard sports original apple-green paint. The oil painting of a farm and barn is by Hannah Stearns.

ABOVE: A versatile craftsman, Art Stearns fashioned twin bed frames from hand-picked sassafras logs. LEFT: The Stearnses reconstructed their 1863 poplar cabin, leaving chinked logs intact and adding a new kitchen wing and a hand-cut picket fence.

Hannah is attracted to things that show wear, choosing the rough over the pristine every time. "If there's something new in the mix, it throws everything off," she says. She also insists on a sense of appropriateness in what she puts together. That's why she avoids collecting multiples of the same thing, because in real life, she points out, early homeowners would never acquire more baskets or bowls, say, than they used in daily tasks.

Her old-fashioned values are reflected in her determination to keep the traditional art of letter-writing alive to sustain her many friendships. "It's become an important part of my life, connecting me to family and friends when we become separated," she says. "It's also been the basis for building new friendships, and sometimes for rekindling a lost one."

Because regular correspondence takes some discipline, Hannah always tries to accomplish some of it before 7 A.M. "I find it's a great way to start the day, quietly 'chatting,'" she says. "Then, during the day, I often jot down notes as I'm working, to include in future letters and cards."

Not surprisingly, she keeps those cards and letters in an appropriate container.

"It's a handsome, soldier-blue, antique sugar bucket which has been filled several times," Hannah says. "I save the unusual cards in a scrapbook that no doubt will be enjoyed by someone long after I'm gone."

LEFT: The staples of an old-fashioned pantry enjoy a renewed shelf life. BELOW: To extend storage capacity in a small bathroom, a rustic plant stand and a set of country baskets were drafted into service. The half shutters, which let in light while protecting privacy, were pieced together from old wooden planks, then antiqued to look weatherbeaten.

LEFT: Early advertising boxes enliven a simple 19th-century cupboard with their colorful slogans. BELOW: A kitchen tableau combines daisies in an old crockery vessel and an inviting slice of apple pie. BELOW LEFT: The hand-painted "antiqued" finish that distinguishes the Stearnses' retail and special-order product line was used to create an impressive Stars and Stripes on a wall in their shop where a fireplace once stood. OPPOSITE: The 1840s mantel is a local find that looks as though it is original to the cabin. Atop, a collection of miniature log cabins includes children's models and a pioneer dwelling complete with sliding "Indian-proof" windows.

A Cloister That Houses Tradition and Spirit

PAINTER **CAROL ANTHONY** grew up in the genteel Connecticut countryside, surrounded by American antiques which her father collected with a passion. She, her twin sister, Elaine, also an artist, and brother Jay were exposed to classic furnishings and art. "It still is what grounds me, being in touch with traditions that have stood the test of time," she says. Then she adds with a laugh, "Even today I don't really own anything 20th century, except ice cube trays!"

Carol's fascination with the past deepened on a sabbatical in England, where she lived for some time in the tower of a 13th-century abbey, her only company the doves nesting in the gargoyles below her window.

Now, however, instead of a bucolic New England setting, or an aerie from the Middle Ages, Carol has created for herself a Southwestern version of a "cloister," as she calls it, on five wild acres near Santa Fe, New Mexico. The compound, with its spectacular views of the Sangre de Cristo Mountains, consists of a 1,300-square-

On a work table, the tools of the artist's trade make an arresting composition. OPPOSITE: Artist Carol Anthony's love of simple, natural things is evident in her collections, from the thrown bowl to an old weatherbeaten Mexican cupboard.

OPPOSITE AND RIGHT: Anthony's collecting habits cover every surface in the casita's kitchen. Her signature studies of pears, apples, and a larger-than-life egg share wall space with the colorful works of fellow artist friends. Even the cookstove, when not fired up, serves as additional gallery space. BELOW: The handiwork of artisans old and new is evoked in an antique carved doorway from Morocco and contemporary screen construction in metal.

foot casita, or "little house," which contains her studio and living quarters, a thatched-roof sanctuary for meditation, and an enchanting walled garden.

"This slice of land," she says, "with its sand and rock, carefully chosen amid four beautiful piñon trees, is a slice of 18th-century time frozen."

Although Carol loves solitude and depends on it to further her art, she has a wide circle of friends and fellow artists. "I built the cloister with friends, some great humor, tequila, and now and then, hugs, money and some delicious ratatouille," she relates.

Both the casita and the chapel were built using straw-bale construction techniques, originally developed by early settlers when lumber became scarce. All the work was done by "The Blue Ravens," a construction company run by two artist friends, painter Jerry West and sculptor Charlie Southard. The straw bales were set into a wood frame, then wrapped in chicken wire. "The straw bales not only define the thickness and strength and curve of the walls," Carol says, "but they lend an old-fashioned warmth and early Southwestern architectural feeling." The

ABOVE: Separating the studio from the living area is a stainless-steel wall-on-wheels, a collaboration by local artists Larry Swann and Margaret Webb. Above one of Carol's paintings hangs a crucifix made in metal. RIGHT: An old frame was converted into a rustic gate with the addition of twiggy pickets. BELOW: Mexican country chairs await a circle of friends.

RIGHT: A collector's fascination for "anything of the earth" is apparent in everything from the array of contemporary clay pieces by Elizabeth MacDonald, arranged in the living area on an old pine table, to the hand-hewn character of the casita itself, built out of dirt, sand, and straw with the collective effort of many friends.

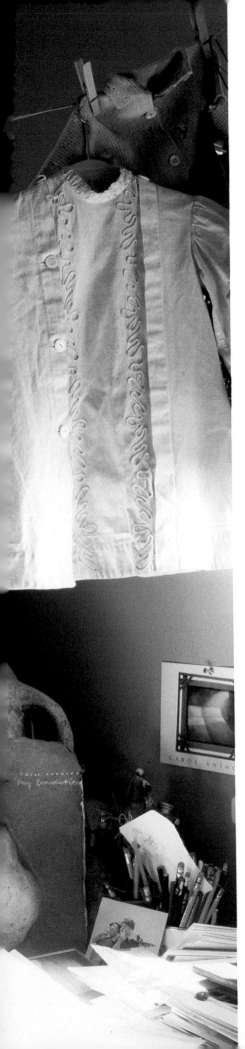

process of covering the walls, called "mudding," is similar to plastering, and involves troweling a mixture of earth, sand, and straw onto the straw to create the wall surfaces.

Inside Carol's casita of straw, her possessions reflect her unique approach to collecting, a blend of bartering, scavenging, and creating that results in what she calls "a natural extension of the spirit within." An antique Mexican desk and testaro share space with a steel daybed made by sculptor friend Larry Swann, amid wonderful Navajo rugs. Her father's teakettles and her sister's pueblo dishes mingle with tiny ceramic sculptures by another friend, Elizabeth MacDonald. New woodwork wears a rustic treatment by Melinda Reed, who specializes in painting furniture so that it looks as old as the hills.

"I'm following my own vision of monastic life here," Carol says. "I accept some 20th-century amenities, such as a phone answering machine or an ice cube tray, because they give me the freedom to live with my 18th-century mud, windows, doors, and columns, the physical environment of a cloister."

The answering machine, turned on from nine to five every day, protects Carol from 20th-century intrusions while she is at her easel, creating her luminous images of timeless landscapes and mystical rooms. Her medium, soft oil pastels on gessoed panels, take on the texture of fresco as she uses her fingertips to blend and knead bits of color.

The paintings Carol creates "are the larger gestures of pilgrimage and solace," says the artist, a collector of time as well as objects, "each mined from the reverie and surreality of the Ancient Moment."

TOP: Simple furnishings with worn surfaces add their ordinary charm to a sleeping area. ABOVE: A work in progress awaits finishing brush strokes in the casita's studio. OPPOSITE: Childhood mementos—baby clothes and early photographs of Carol with her parents and twin sister, Elaine— are cleverly displayed for all to enjoy.

The Queen of **Lean**

THE COLLECTOR'S HABITAT is often a place densely layered with furnishings, artwork, and objects. The home of interior designer Ellen Windham is the opposite. Avoiding clutter and confusion in every room, she prefers to do more with less.

Ellen works wonders in small ways. Exploiting the available niches, mantels, ledges, and tabletops found in a room, she creates vignettes for the eye, pleasing arrangements that tease, tantalize, and inspire. The results show what can be done with small collected things when a sense of balance, proportion, and design is put to work. Ellen often combines disparate items from the ends of the earth to bring out qualities that would not have been noticed if the objects were displayed separately. An icon from Old Russia shares her mantel with a gilded mirror from Peru. In her entry, an old Mexican pine cabinet is dressed with an Indian rug, while on the wall, two vintage portraits of children play counterpoint to a Mexican cross

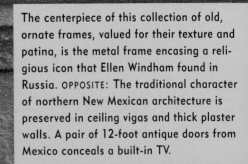

The centerpiece of this collection of old, ornate frames, valued for their texture and patina, is the metal frame encasing a religious icon that Ellen Windham found in Russia. OPPOSITE: The traditional character of northern New Mexican architecture is preserved in ceiling vigas and thick plaster walls. A pair of 12-foot antique doors from Mexico conceals a built-in TV.

ABOVE: Adobe walls and a cowhide rug make a suitable staging area for painted country pieces and a rush-seat chair. BELOW: Displaying a collection of like things, such as frames all made of silver, increases the impact that small objects can make in a room.

painted with a religious scene depicting the soul emerging from Purgatory.

"I don't buy a thing unless I have a clear idea where I might use it," she says, adding that the beauty of small things is that they are easier to find a roost for in the house than large furniture. For her house, she is always on the lookout for old silver, black-and-white photographs, picture frames, and antique religious art and artifacts, such as the folk art figure of a guardian angel from the Philippines that sits atop her bedpost. "I like surprise and whimsy," she says, "little touches here and there that make people laugh."

Little things are easier to move and change, too. A friend calls her "the Queen of Lean" because of her penchant for leaning pictures against any available vertical surfaces. She stacks her pictures and portraits, instead of hanging them in fixed locations, so that when she tires of the first one in line, she can switch it with another. Periodically, she changes the things that grace her tabletops and shelves.

Another example of the designer's restraint is the fact that she only used two kinds of upholstery fabrics in the house. A collection of old textiles helped her introduce color, pattern, and texture. A bed is strikingly layered with an Indian dhurrie and a New Mexico satillo blanket. Pillows in the living room are fashioned from Native American weavings and assorted vintage rug remnants.

"A house should reflect your personality and contain the things you love," says Ellen. "But too much of a good thing leads to confusion, I think. Keeping it simple is the best rule of thumb for me. Simple, interesting, and fun."

Ellen experienced an aesthetic sea change when she moved to Santa Fe from

ABOVE: Worn wood surfaces and old weavings from the owner's collection of Mexican antiques provide the motif for a lively living room scheme.

Texas, where she had been an avid collector of contemporary ceramics. "In Dallas, my interiors were white, very minimal, with contemporary art and ceramics," she observes. "But that look was too cool for me out here. In Santa Fe, I was drawn to the old things, the warm things." Her interest in the old religious art of Mexico and New Mexico was piqued not by religion, but by the ancient patina of the pieces, many with elaborate gold leafing on them. And yet, "I had wanted to surround myself with things that had meant something to someone." The element of personal meaning gives a collected piece more than just aesthetic value.

Ellen lives only five minutes from downtown Santa Fe, on land she fell in love with because it affords spectacular views of a dramatic ski basin and the Badlands to the north. She built her house in stages. It is constructed in the shape of a cross and

LEFT: An outsized old mirror frame holds a group of contemporary black-and-white photographs, juxtaposed with a Madonna and Child in a rustic frame. Stacking rather than hanging art enables one to change collections on a whim. RIGHT: Watched over by a guardian angel, a bed is dressed in a Mexican Saltillo and Indian dhurrie, with antique lace shams for a touch of elegance. BELOW LEFT: Bibelots such as perfume flacons, lidded vanity jars, boxes, and vases lend their silvery beauty to the bath.

has the tin roof and adobe walls traditional to northern New Mexico, with a skylight at the apex of the roof. Windows and exterior doors are contemprary, while within, there are old doors from Mexico and ceilings with vigas and latillas.

"I found the adobe architecture and plaster walls very conducive to bringing together things from many different origins," she says. And as an inveterate traveler, Ellen has been to many of the origins. She never returns from a trip empty-handed, but always with something to introduce into some nook or cranny back home.

Ellen visited Moscow shortly after the collapse of the Soviet Union. She discovered that huge flea markets had sprung up overnight in the first chaotic months of the new free-market economy. "Nobody in bazaars knew what the rules were, and nobody had any money," she recalls, "but everybody was trying to sell something." The merchandise she found there ranged from large commercial appliances to venerable icons.

Ellen had no use for a bulky icebox. But she found an authentic religious icon to take home, at $30 an astounding bargain.

the eclectic Decorator

Antiques purists may surround themselves with nothing but authentic furnishings from one particular period or style, but most collectors do not have that luxury. In some ways, an eclectic collection, borrowing freely from many periods and styles, has more lasting interest, with its potential for ever changing and evolving in character. This form of collecting has its own discipline, too, for it is governed by the tastes and preferences of the collector, and is not a result of accumulating things with an "anything goes" mentality.

A one-note collection can wear thin. It may have been fun to assemble a dozen or so folk images of cows, for example, but such a collection cannot form the basis for furnishing a room agreeably. A more broadly based collection, for example one that springs from a common rural tradition, is versatile. A painted country cupboard, a metal garden chair, a Navajo rug, an Amish shawl, and an apple basket can fill an urban habitat with unified country style.

When eclectic collections have a common thread, they give rooms a unique decorative stamp. "I like the look of off-white slipcovers set off by the lines of well-made wooden pieces around them," notes Maine dealer Barbara Doherty. Here are other ideas for organizing your collections.

Keep backgrounds simple. Paint rooms in neutral colors, such as Decorator White by Benjamin Moore. The colors, patterns, and textures of beloved objects will stand out more against a plain setting.

Unify artwork by theme. If you are drawn to vintage black-and-white photographs, limit what you collect to only portraits, say, or beach scenes, or city life. The handiwork of amateur Sunday painters looks more masterly if the examples are all floral—a grouping of studies of roses, for example, may be quite effective even though no single picture is a work of art. Botanical studies can be brought together similarly.

Unify artwork by the way you frame it. Pictures of different subjects can be grouped more easily if similar frame materials are used. Gilt frames, ornately carved frames, rustic twig frames, or contemporary museum-style frames all can be used to coordinate a varied art gallery without it appearing chaotic.

Use vintage textiles to renew interiors. Santa Fe interior designer Ellen Windham prefers to limit upholstery fabrics to a few neutral choices, and let "my collection of old weavings provide all the pattern and interest." It's easier to introduce new pillows made from remnants of kilim rugs, forties fabrics, or homespun than to reupholster all the furniture. Collect old furniture frames and cover them in solid or neutral textured fabrics, then let old textiles add the eye appeal in smaller, decorative touches. Rotate your Beacon blankets, quilts,

ethnic weavings, and paisley throws for seasonal variety.

Focusing a collection around furniture such as cupboards or chairs can add visual interest and utility to a house. For instance, several cupboards can do the job of cabinets in a kitchen or dining room. Or, there are always corners or empty walls for small chairs to fill, with the fetching details of their construction, making an eye-catching design.

Painted furniture pieces may come from different eras, but the quality and texture of their surfaces can tie them together in appealing groupings. Patina is the common denominator.

Collect little things such as silver objects, tole ware, or painted boxes, and use them to decorate tabletops and shelves. "Instead of moving around major pieces of furniture, I change out things on tabletops or shelves to give my rooms a fresh look," adds Ellen Windham.

Make a favorite color scheme the subject of a collection. Warm blue-and-white combinations can be found in a wide range of materials: fabrics such as quilts, toile, and ticking, pottery and china, milk-painted furniture, and dhurrie rugs, just to name a few. Placed in the same room, they bring instant color coordination to the space.

Contemporary classics and timeless antiques also make good bedfellows. "Design is what appeals to me in old pieces as well as new," says Santa Fe dealer Gloria List, who forty years ago dared to put her first really good antique—"a walnut chest which I still have"—next to a stark, sleek Herman Miller sofa. Because both pieces had quality lines and design, the pairing was a visual success.

Finally, the heritage of the region where one lives can be drawn on to give meaning to a collection. If many things in the house bear the hand of local artisans and artists, chances are they will evoke a common vision spanning many decades, and will make for a beautiful collection of history.

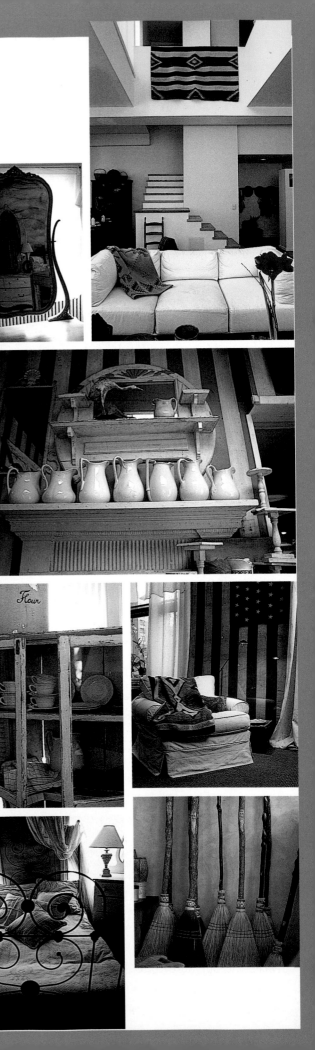

Twin Cabins
of Authenticity

THE IDEA FOR SKIPPER and Olga Bowles's collection of family and regional treasures was born in a log cabin. When Skipper was a boy, he and his siblings had the run of an old log cabin on their family's property in rural North Carolina. Long abandoned, it served alternately as clubhouse, fort, secret hiding place, and pony stable for the youngsters. These were idyllic times for the city-raised Skipper, who grew up in Greensboro, North Carolina, the son of a state senator and financial consultant. The cabin was all that remained of the Bowles family's country ties. "Like many Southerners, we're only one generation removed from the country," Skipper adds.

Years later, while quail hunting in a field north of Greensboro, Skipper stumbled upon an empty log cabin that triggered those early childhood memories of his cherished haunt. Built in the traditional Southern "dog-trot" style, with a

Log cabins dating from 1790 and 1860 were restored by Skipper and Olga Bowles, who saved the original plain oak and pine walls as the perfect backdrop for their collection of regional and inherited antiques, such as the paint-decorated chairs and country table in the dining room, OPPOSITE, and the North Carolina corner chair and Georgia settle in the sunroom.

wide center hall running from front to back, the 1860 cabin seemed too good to be true. Skipper set out to track down its owner. "The farmer was happy to part with the decrepit cabin for $2,500," recalls Skipper, but it wasn't until he met his future wife, Olga, that he would fulfill his country dream. "I needed the right partner and the right place to do it," he says.

The right place was a 112-acre site just outside a tiny village in northwestern South Carolina, near Greenville, where Skipper was then living and working as a stockbroker. "We knew we wanted the property the first time we saw it," says Olga, The one-time cotton farm had been dubbed "Red Hill" by the slaves who originally worked the land (whose descendants are now friends and neighbors), for the color of its clay soil and its historic hilltop location. A recent archaeological dig just off the property revealed Native American artifacts dating to 450 A.D. The site was long overgrown, but "the view was there, even with all the trees," she adds. What wasn't there was a second log cabin. "We saw that one cabin wasn't going to be big enough for us, so we started searching for a second one and found it in York County, South Carolina," says Skipper. This cabin, also abandoned, dated from 1790.

Olga diligently kept a scrapbook recording the eighteen-month process of disassembling, relocating, and rebuilding the log cabins on their present site. "Crews of carpenters and stonemasons put the cabins back together like so many Lincoln Logs," she says. The foundation

and hearths were built with native stone trucked in from the mountains of North Carolina and then laid by hand. Once merged, the two cabins formed a T: the North Carolina cabin welcoming visitors in front and the South Carolina cabin set behind it. Two one-story clapboard additions with sloping roofs square off the whole cabin and cover the open sides. The traditional mortar chinking that gives the hand-hewn log walls their authentic cabin style also conceals any evidence of modern insulation.

Bowles family furnishings anchor the

ABOVE: An oil portrait of Margaret Thomas, Skipper Bowles's great-grandmother, oversees old gathering baskets on and under a hunt board. LEFT: The vintage gas pump was installed as a colorful accessory for the metal-roofed outbuilding. OPPOSITE: The catch of the day, direct from the stocked farm pond, is at home in a kitchen furnished with an 1840 milk cupboard with tin panels, an 1880 primitive walnut corner cupboard, and an 1870–80 rustic table with original blue paint, all made in North Carolina.

In the spacious main room, an enthusiasm for wildfowl takes flight in a collection of mounted trophies and decoys. A prized Tennessee rifle from the 1800s is over the mantel. The glass-doored corner cupboard was made in North Carolina. OPPOSITE: Beds from the owner's childhood years, made from walnut harvested on a paternal grandparent's farm in Bristol, Virginia, are dressed with North Carolina quilts.

interiors of the cabin in the reality of another time. Two 19th-century beds in the guest room are hewn from walnut cut on the mountainous land in southwest Virginia that Skipper's great-grandparents originally farmed. An old family tea service has taken up a dainty holding position on the antique sideboard in the dining room, under a stern portrait of Skipper's great-great-grandfather, who served as a colonel in the Confederate Army. Elsewhere, other ancestor portraits and 19th-century samplers mingle with the mounted wildlife trophies that are a tribute to Skipper's sportsman skills. And, to accommodate a 1790 walnut corner cupboard inherited from Skipper's great-grandmother, the couple went so far as to have the first floor ceiling raised the height of one log.

Authenticity guided the consolidation of the two cabins, from the choice of doors and doorknobs ("I found a collection of old doors in a local antiques shop and then had to buy forty sets of knobs and locks to assemble twelve that worked," notes Olga) to the period window pulls and hinges reproduced by a blacksmith.

The allure of the countryside has been a magnet for generations of the Bowles family. "All the Bowleses are from the country," Skipper says, "and one by one we've gotten back." With 100 acres of woodland and a 3-acre pond, the twin cabin property of Skipper and Olga is the center of a year-long wildlife preserve, for wood ducks, Canadian geese, quail, and an occasional wild turkey. "I'm much more of a conservationist now," says Skipper, whose sport these days leans more toward raising and enjoying wildlife and hunting antiques.

Good, Better, **Best!**

F IT IS THE DUTY OF DEALERS to size up an object for price and provenance, it is the collector's inclination to give more attention to its esthetic value and its historic setting.

One such collector, Richard Levey, breathes life into objects by trying to understand their origins and purposes. "It has much to do with how I was raised," he believes. With a father who was an architect and a mother educated at the London School of Economics, Richard grew up in an intellectually challenging atmosphere, "a 'salon,' of sorts, where inquiry and curiosity were encouraged. Writers and artists were frequent dinner and house guests, and, like every inquisitive young child, I just eavesdropped— and then, as I grew, was welcomed into those 'Round Table' discussions. Visiting writers often inscribed copies of their books for me, and one artist carved a book-as-object . . . and two collections were born."

"I don't think people always start

A highly decorated and whimsically carved and painted candlestand, circa 1880, holds a painted trinket box from the Lipman Collection and two wooden dancing toys. OPPOSITE: In the entrance hall of the Levey home in Michigan, a one-drawer, cut-wood wall shelf with deer silhouette displays a santos figure, while a mid-19th-century Scandinavian table with blue-green legs holds a paint-decorated treen jar from the 1840s and a pre-1900 Scandinavian pottery bowl with stone fruit.

Social realist Ben Shahn's portrait of U.S. Senators Arthur H. Vanderburg, Thomas E. Dewey, and Robert A. Taft overlooks a painted dry sink holding painted treen jars, a tole tray and matching salt and pepper shakers, and a small part of Richard Levey's collection of bottle whimsies. The chair with split-wood caned seat is one of a set of twelve attributed to an Ohio Shaker community. OPPOSITE: The folk art enlivening a Pennsylvania dough table circa 1840 includes a salesman's sample ladder, a Jesus-in-a-bottle whimsy with a stopper carved in the form of a church steeple, and a carved open book. The luminous still life is by Joseph Glover (b. 1906).

out intending to collect things they really love or learn to love," he continues, suggesting that the process is more organic and subject to chance. "It's as if you happen upon, fall in love with, and acquire a tramp-art picture frame; then you chance upon and acquire another one . . . and suddenly you have started a collection."

Richard's eclectic collection of books-as-objects began in earnest in the mid-'70s when he acquired a carved piece of walnut burl, stamped "Lizzie Jones/Born Feb/The First/1883/in Kenton, Ohio," which turned out to be a memorial tribute. Since then, he has amassed several hundred books-as-objects, including trinket, match, and needle cases; Napoleonic prisoner-of-war art; sample pieces by itinerant tombstone carvers; "devil's bibles"; end-of-the-day sewer tile and coal carvings; clay flasks; a parson's pitch pipe; and one box carved by a Wisconsin State Prison inmate to hold his coinage tokens.

Bottle whimsies are another focus of Richard's unique collecting impulse. This collection includes many examples of Jesus-in-a-bottle, "find the hidden man," furniture-in-a-bottle, and cedar-fans-in-a-bottle. "I have one that portrays a marital drama involving a sea captain, his wife, first mate, and a rooster. The first mate is presenting himself to the wife, but the flirtation is hidden from the captain by the rooster." However, not every bottle whimsy passes his criteria. "The craftsmanship has to be superior, and I prefer bottles with carved stoppers. I have several with a stopper carved in the form of a hand holding a book—and, quite naturally, I'm looking for others by the same carver."

In the late 1960s, Richard's eye was taken with paint-decorated furniture. "For me, there were two forms of paint-decorated furniture: the kind that makes

no bones about letting you know it's painted—with stencils, birds, vines, unicorns, and the like—and the kind that is in the spirit of trompe l'oeil, where pine or other common wood was painted to simulate the 'more desirable' cherry, walnut burl, or maple."

He became intrigued with the way old furniture made it through the years or fell by the wayside. "Many old and wonderful pieces survive because they landed in an attic or barn. When families came into money, they filled the house with the fashions of the day and put the old stuff away," he explains. "But if the pieces remained in heavy daily service in families who were not wealthy, these tended to succumb to wear and tear, or they were stripped and refinished, tinkered with, or they just broke and were not repaired."

Senna kilim rugs and an Amish quilt made in Holmes County, Ohio, in 1908 lend warmth to the master bedroom. The exceptional three-color Halley's Comet blanket chest dates from about 1845. Painted Indiana Amish plant stands, dated 1911, and a Shaker wooden apple carrier evoke the rural past, while the countertop advertising figure on the mantel is a token of early commerce. A pair of wooden prickets, a painted wooden book box, and a niche from New Mexico, circa 1890, also grace the mantel.

For dealers, good business practice dictates a "here today, gone tomorrow" philosophy regarding their precious inventory. Time is on the side of a collector like Richard in his patient quest to create a superlative collection. Like all serious collectors, he and his wife, Sigrid Christiansen, believe there is a hierarchy of value and quality associated with virtually all categories of antiques. It's seldom enough to attain "good." Collectors are driven to upgrade to "better" and "best."

"We try to distance ourselves from those collectors who first can't live without it and then can't live with it comfortably—especially those who regale you with stories about how little they paid for a great but impractical object. We have two young boys (both of whom have caught the collecting bug), and we have to live every day with our finds," he observes. "We strive to find the best and most comfortable and usable examples. I can appreciate a Samuel Gragg chair just fine at Greenfield Village or on the printed page. There is absolutely no point in our owning an object so precious and fragile. It should go in a collection where it fits . . . and hopefully one where it can be enjoyed by the public."

It is not surprising that the early Utopian societies that settled in the East and Midwest have long fascinated Richard. "The Zoarists, the New Harmony-ites, the Amish—all had great traditions of making simple, functional furnishings and other household items," he points out. "These communities were a lot like the Shakers in their goal to be totally self-sufficient and removed from the world. The Utopian-society furniture works extremely well for us . . . and we are saddened that the furniture has outlived the concept and the reality of the Utopian communities themselves."

the tale of the Tag

The price of an antique is subject to many different factors, some of which fluctuate with time and fashion. Here are the most important things that give value to an antique:

RARITY. American furniture from the 1600s is rare because there was never that much of it to go around. Virtually every stick of furniture that the original settlers of the colonies sat on, slept in, or ate at is in museums or historic houses today. More recent antiques may be rare because only a few specimens were made or only a few examples survive.

STYLE, BEAUTY, AND QUALITY OF DESIGN. Antiques with strong aesthetic properties are superior to similar pieces made by lesser craftsmen.

CONDITION. Some collectors don't mind possessing flawed pieces—a ceramic bowl with a hairline crack, a cupboard with one of its original drawers replaced, a fabric with a tear or stain—because they feel the pieces have the added charm of having been used. However, the bottom line is that an antique in pristine condition is more valuable than its shopworn cousin.

PROVENANCE. An antique once owned by a famous person or family tends to accumulate more value than a similar piece that never enjoyed a brush with celebrity.

POPULARITY. Mainstream fads and fashions affect the value of antiques by altering the equation of supply and demand. When the American Bicentennial was observed in 1976, there was an outpouring of interest in the objects of early national life, such as quilts and folk art, which automatically made those objects more expensive. Keeping ahead of the trends is a key to success in the business. After specializing in quilts in the 1970s, with good results, Santa Fe dealer Gloria List moved into Native American arts and crafts in the 1980s. As that market matured, she shifted in the 1990s into the religious art of New Mexico, Mexico, Spain, and Central and South America.

Those are the general ingredients that go into an antique's selling price, all of which the dealer is well aware of. Additionally, the dealer is influenced by the price he or she paid for the piece. If the stake is high and there are bills to pay, the dealer may be willing to let the antique go for a bargain price. Alternatively, the dealer may be in a position to hold on to the piece until market conditions favor a more profitable asking price. Often, the vigor of the economy and the "action" in the antiques marketplace will dictate the dealer's strategy.

Other factors that figure in the dealer's calculations are the antique's book value, or what similar pieces are known to be going for, and overhead (dealers who do business through shows have heavy expenses, and shop operators have fixed monthly costs).

With all these variables, it's not surprising that three almost identical antiques might show up in the market with three different prices. Antiques are worth whatever someone is willing to pay for them. That doesn't mean the price on the tag is some wild invention of a dealer, however.

For all these reasons, it is advisable to think twice before making some preposterously low offer on an antique that you come upon. A polite "Can you take less for this item?" or "Is the price firm?" is more likely to fall on receptive ears.

"You can go for the short markup, and sell something every day," observes Midwestern dealer Rod Lich, "or stick to your price and bide your time. Personally, I'd rather do a lot of shows and move a lot of pieces than sit tight on my inventory in a shop for weeks at a time."

Faith in the
Original Design

MARY AND MARC
Cooper call them-
selves "impurists,
not purists" when it
comes to collecting, but the effect is
pure magic in the couple's raised
center-hall Victorian cottage, circa
1885, in New Orleans, Louisiana.

"The house assembles the past
and present in a 'living' home that
is gracious and elegant, yet simple
and hospitable," notes Marc. It
allows authentic period furnishings
to commingle with later fashions of
the day, such as the 1940s Sears &
Roebuck mixing bowls that fill the
original kitchen shelves.

"Nothing we collect is strictly decorative or whimsical," adds Mary.
The Sears mass-market pottery, for
example, is charming with its cattail
design details, but eminently useful
for cooking. Mary continues, "I have
to find things for almost nothing,
because I do use them," including
the vintage linen sheets which they
sleep on every night.

First-time visitors to the Coopers'
New Orleans house are usually

Antique footed bowls and a pair of wreaths share a common botanical theme. OPPOSITE: The blue-green "pond-like" Shearwater pottery was crafted in an Ocean City, Mississippi, pottery works across the street from a former residence of Mary Cooper.

struck by an absence of modern conveniences. There is no dishwasher, microwave, or air-conditioning; they take advantage of the tall ceilings, double-hung sash windows, louvred shutters, and ceiling fans to stay cool. Mary admits, however, to keeping a TV stored on a rolling stand in the only closet in the house. She likes to equate this to a favorite Gary Larsen "Far Side" cartoon in which, she says, "the village natives are in their thatched huts frantically hiding their televisions and microwaves and the caption underneath reads, 'The anthropologists are coming!

The anthropologists are coming!'"

"Our goal has been to keep the house authentic and still make compromises for modern living, hoping that the compromises have been few," says Marc. "The whole idea of an old house is that it is different. You have to peel back the layers and put your faith in the original design, instead of reinventing the wheel."

The family's fidelity to the past is reflected in Mary's chair restoration business and Marc's job as director of the Vieux Carré Commission, which works to protect the architecture of the historic French Quarter. Their daughter, Jennifer, a graduate student of printmaking, collects 1950s decorative arts and dice.

Before the Coopers rescued their cottage it had been vacant so long that a pack of wild dogs were living under it. "When we looked at it, I thought it was far too much work and we would be crazy to get

LEFT: Marc Cooper collects old lattice boxes and other containers fashioned from thin strips of Spanish cedar, an aromatic wood used to make cigar boxes. BELOW: Understated antiques such as the sofa made in 1840 in Natchez, Mississippi, enhance the dwelling's Creole character. Suspended from the restored picture molding is a period reversed copper engraving known as an optique. The ceiling fan and louvered shutters are not just decorative but necessary in the Louisiana heat. OPPOSITE: A grouping of 19th-century plant studies stands out in the master bedroom, which is painted in "Paris Green," the old pharmacist's euphemism for "powdered arsenic."

involved with this project," recalls Mary.

But they were swayed by the undeveloped expanse that came with the urban location, a very tempting area for Mary's gardening ambitions. They also were captivated by the restrained architecture. "It was much simpler than other houses of this period," notes Mary, and more suited to their '"unvarnished" style.

There were unexpected hidden assets as well. "We wouldn't have our mochaware collection if it weren't for the fact that this house had been relocated to its present site around 1907," says Marc. "The front gallery sits over a privvy that served an earlier house, and under that, we found pottery shards. Mary glued the mochaware back together." Battered but not beaten, the pottery is presently displayed on the shelves of a locally made cypress breakfront, which probably came out of a church rectory. "When we found this old piece," Marc reasons, "there was a cardboard sign on the back with the word 'Psalms' written on it."

Anything that comes into the Cooper house has to have some old-fashioned feeling. This applies to everything from paint colors, such as the dark green used on the dining room walls—matched to a chunk of the original plaster—to early toilet-paper dispensers, which Marc collects. "These were used by the plumbers to advertise their services," he explains. "They were usually cast in brass with the name, address, and phone number of the plumber on them. They sometimes featured a motto as well." Marc's favorite occupies a place of honor in one of the bathrooms. "Plumbers Who Work With A Vim," is the message engraved on brass. If you had to devise a motto for the Coopers, it might be: "Collectors Who Collect With Vim And Vigor."

An uncommon color palette yields a feeling of déja vù to the interiors. OPPOSITE, ABOVE: In the dining room, walls were painted to match the color found in a piece of original plaster, calling attention to an impressive cypress breakfront. OPPOSITE, BELOW LEFT. A collection of celluloid silhouettes provided the black and cream color scheme for the bathroom. OPPOSITE, BELOW RIGHT: The terra-cotta walls were inspired by the color of ripe pomegranates found in Mary Cooper's backyard garden. ABOVE: Carved, polished, or left plain, antique wood surfaces infuse the house with authenticity. BELOW: In keeping with the period of the house when closets did not exist, a diminutive armoire, originally for a child's room, solves storage needs of today.

Emblems of the wild and frontier
handiwork surround a primitive
cupboard from Maine in a Berkshire Mountains outpost of Americana. OPPOSITE: Icons of farm and
range—baskets, buckets, and cupboards with peeling paint—bring
the spirit of the pioneering past to
the home of collectors Tasha and
Jack Polizzi, created by joining a
pair of 18th-century barns.

A Comfortable and Venerable Homestead

DEEP IN THE HEART OF THE Berkshire Mountains of western Massachusetts, Tasha and Jack Polizzi have turned a pair of old barns, joined at the hip, into a comfortable homestead that is also a showcase for their wild taste in collecting.

The oldest part of the dwelling dates from the 1790s and has the massive proportions one expects of a former working barn. With towering native stone hearths and chinked, split-log walls, it is the ideal setting for Tasha's collection of rustic furniture and wilderness artifacts. The omnipresent wood surfaces made it all but certain that Tasha would decorate the house using primitive and rustic pieces, such as the country breakfront in the dining room that is filled with her collection of 19th-century buttermilk-painted bowls.

"My dad was an avid outdoorsman," Tasha relates, explaining her deeply felt affinity for relics of the woods and the range. "As a kid I loved to go hunting and fishing with him." Years later, her career in the

Collections dominate in the
living room: early Navajo
rugs, one a First Phase
Chief's blanket, drape sofas
with a vivid field of color
and pattern. Old slipware
plates, Navajo wedding baskets and pottery, and framed
images of the frontier find a
natural perch on the mantel.
Textile odds and ends such
as old Mexican serapes and
vintage blowsy chintz have
been recycled to cover pillows. A fire screen, branded
with Tasha's initials, was
fashioned from discarded
horseshoes.

LEFT: Old paint and Old Glory, used as a window swag, brighten a corner in the dining room. Hues of harvested natural materials blend companionably with the colors of old painted surfaces. RIGHT: A unique work of art, a Canadian mooseskin etched with the natural wonders of the northern woods, is signed, dated 1916, and titled *Reclamation*. A table covered with an old Pendleton blanket is flanked by a pair of 1920s leather club chairs from England. BELOW: A Navajo chief's blanket, dated 1910, makes an imposing wall hanging.

fashion business as both model and executive made Tasha realize her strong love of the outdoors extended to appreciating the finer things one wore to survive in style in the wild. "Once I stepped into a pair of hand-tooled cowboy boots," she admits, "I never stepped out."

Her next step was to extend that passion into an enterprise. In 1990 she opened T. P. Saddleblanket & Trading, Inc., in a corner storefront in Great Barrington, Massachusetts, stocking it with Western-themed memorabilia and rough-hewn Americana. "It is my guilt-free excuse for feeding my buying and collecting urges," she jokes about the business, which also includes a clothing line of her own design—camp-blanket skirts, hand-painted denim shirts, and velvet jackets with a fun Western swagger.

Tasha and Jack began collecting rustic furniture and cowboy relics more than fifteen years ago. "We bought with our hearts and our eyes," she recalls, "not looking at it as an 'investment.'" Today, their home is a veritable mini-museum of primitive Americana, filled to the rafters with objects found near and far, from the Adirondacks in New York State to the

A cache of Western souvenirs trims a heart-shaped wreath on the kitchen mantel, where antique beaded Indian moccasins hang from the chimney. Vintage trade blankets and Navajo weavings create a bold color scheme dominated by red, orange, black, and white.

Michigan woods to the Southwestern desert. At first, Jack was a step behind Tasha in the pursuit. "When she started bringing home beat-up furniture with peeling paint," he admits, "I remember thinking, 'Oh, no! Not that old thing!'"

Under its beamed ceiling, the living room in the Polizzi house is a visual feast, layer after layer of time and tradition. The fireplace mantel is alive with tribal treasures—ceremonial Navajo wedding baskets, vintage photos of the Wild West, weavings and pottery—offset by enduring New England icons like a redware plate and a weathervane. Elsewhere, the house resembles a venerable wilderness camp. There are Beacon blankets, birch bowls, miniature tepees, tomtoms, animal pelts, and antler racks. One very rare Canadian moose skin is etched with a deep woods scene that captures the romantic fascination of the chase—and the ungainly beauty of the moose.

The couple's collections are never more resplendent or in evidence than at Christmas. That's when antique sleighbells jingle, old spurs jangle, and beaded buckskin moccasins are hung by the kitchen chimney with care. One year, the Christmas tree in the family room was decorated with found wild turkey feathers, Tasha's turquoise jewelry, other tribal souvenirs, and a feather headdress. Another year it might be chili peppers and cowboy hats: no two Christmases are alike. There's no

tinsel or candy canes here. "Nothing we use to decorate with during the holidays is newly bought," Tasha notes.

The Polizzis bought the Berkshires property in 1979 as the family's weekend retreat. Now it's their permanent residence. Jack can joke about the move from New York City, where he had worked as an executive recruiter, saying "T. P. Saddleblanket rescued me from wearing a three-piece suit." Instead of taxis, the family tootles around in a red 1946 Dodge pickup truck. For sons Christopher and John, the move has been especially rewarding, providing them with backdoor skiing and front door sightings. "Last year, we had a bear in our front yard!" exclaims Chris.

ABOVE: Nineteenth-century buttermilk-painted wooden mixing bowls and other serviceable antiques show their true colors in the dining room. LEFT: In a house where America's past is always present, the pageantry of Christmas has an eclectic feeling. The Saltillo weaving is from an old Adirondack health spa.

care and feeding of Antiques

If cared for properly, antiques and vintage collectibles only get better with age. Here are some housekeeping practices to prevent damage and loss of your prized possessions.

HEAT AND HUMIDITY. Excessive heat or cold is hard on furnishings. Never place antique pieces next to or in front of blasts of hot or frigid air. Heat and humidity are most threatening to textiles, wood surfaces, books, prints, and ephemera. Dampness breeds mildew, dry rot, and fungi. Fungi cause "foxing," the discoloration of old paper. Moisture can loosen glue, warp wood, and buckle paper. The ideal range for humidity in interiors is 30 to 40 percent. Depending on the climate or the season, you can use humidifiers or air conditioners to keep the air in that range.

LIGHT. The ultraviolet light present in both sunlight and fluorescent lights can cause long-term discoloration and damage to sun-sensitive materials. Curtains, blinds, shades, and ultraviolet screening material protect carpets, woodwork, furniture, art, and fabrics from the harsh effects of natural light pouring through windows. To keep the effects of interior lighting in check, rotate antiques and artwork occasionally, and turn your carpets.

DUST. Regular vacuuming of upholstery and carpets will remove dust and dirt that could lead to discoloration and other damage. It may be enough just to shake out small carpets, but avoid "snapping" them as you do so, for an antique might come apart in your hands.

BASKETS. Preserve old baskets simply by spraying them once a year, or every two years, with light furniture oil, or sponging them down with a solution of 40 percent castor oil and 60 percent alcohol, wiping off any excess with a clean, soft cloth.

TEXTILES. Delicate textiles should be handled especially carefully. Hand wash linens, cotton, and wool with a pH-balanced soap or nondetergent soap. It may take several deep rinses to remove all the cleanser. Coverlets, quilts, and handwork are best left unironed. Store with a minimum number of gentle folds, padding the folds with unbleached muslin or acid-free tissue paper.

SILVER. Lightly tarnished plain silver can be rejuvenated with a silver polishing cloth. Ornate silver will clean up better in a silver dip, which removes tarnish without abrading. The slightest amount of moisture will oxidize silver, so, after polishing, blow your silver pieces dry with a hair dryer.

Overly enthusiastic cleaning of antique wood can be more detrimental than a little benign neglect. Regular dusting with a clean, soft cloth is all that most antiques require. Avoid the plethora of "wood care" products on the market. Most of them make the wood look good only momentarily, and some leave an unappealing film on the surface. A once-a-year application of a good paste wax will penetrate the wood, restore its natural gloss, and keep it from drying out.

Dealer's Choice

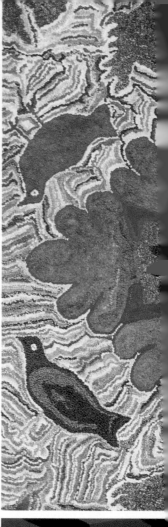

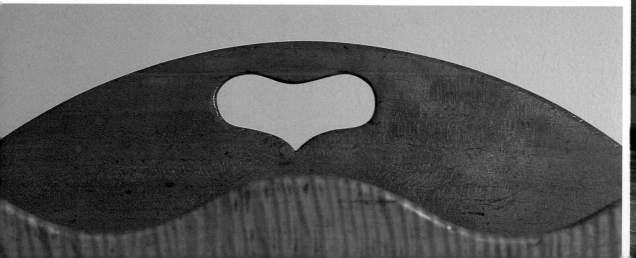

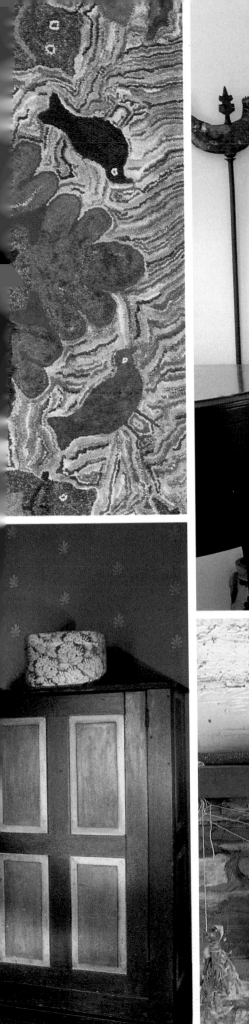

"Most scouts specialize, but not me. I'm too curious, too restless, too much in love with the treasure hunt. I keep on the move constantly, covering as much as I can of the vast grid of dealers, collectors, accumulators, pack rats, antique shops, thrift shops, junk shops, estate sales, country auctions, bankruptcy sales, antique shows, flea markets, and garage sales that covers America like a screen. . . . I fall in love with objects, each in its turn, my only problem being that as I get older, I also get pickier. First-rate objects don't excite me anymore: I want exceptional objects, and those can take a lot of looking for."

—*Cadillac Jack*, by Larry McMurtry

Like the amiable "picker" in Larry McMurtry's novel, dealers are in the business of finding and selling beautiful things. Items flow through their shops and houses, an endless ever-changing parade of shape and color and form, objects with stories to tell or secrets to keep. Living with your inventory does have its inconveniences, though—sometimes you have a kitchen table and sometimes you don't. But the dealer is a veteran at making do until something better, something more wonderful comes along.

Dealers can take a scatter-shot approach to their business, grabbing up anything that smacks of a find, or be incredibly focused, staking cut their territories—baskets, pewter, painted furniture pre-1830—with the eagle eye of a museum curator.

Like Cadillac Jack, dealers are gypsies. The wander the face of the earth. For them, it is the search or the quest that is the thrill. Sometimes the quest is for a specific item—a transferware pattern that one of their

clients collects. But more often than not they are looking for that diamond in the rough—the bargain. Experience and a knowing eye give them the knowledge and the confidence to act upon their discoveries. Some dealers plan their itineraries like a military campaign, hitting every major show, estate sale, and auction. Others are more footloose, allowing whim and happenstance to guide their journey, relying on serendipity to help them come home with the prize.

Possessing the soul of a collector, dealers, too, become attached to art, furnishings, and other objects that come into their grasp. But they are serial lovers. One day it is the Amish quilt, the next the Sheraton chair, and then the gilded mirror. It is this constant ebb and flow of things that imbue the habitats of dealers with a quirky style that never fails to surprise. Just when I think I've seen it all, I'll be brought up by an original idea such as a collection of mismatched carved mirrors hung in the bathroom of an 18th-century house, or the wit that allows piggybanks, WPA paintings, chrome furniture, and Scottish antiques to commingle under one roof.

Dealers have taught me a lot about style over the years, that it's okay to break all the rules and, yes, you can indulge your passion for period styles, but you don't have to live in a museum.

Susie and Richard Burmann revived old paint techniques such as stencilling and floor painting; the quilt-inspired treatment of the floor uses five different colors. OPPOSITE: The painted floors even travel up the staircase.

Using Fine Country
Character and Style

PREBLE **C**OUNTY LIES IN THE heart of Ohio hog-farming country, west of Dayton, north of Cincinnati. It is an area with a mix of architectural styles, some old and restored, others new and trying hard to fit in. Surrounding all the farms is flat land for as far as the eye can see.

"A lot of people don't see the flats as beautiful, but I appreciate the uninterrupted horizons and the long vistas," says Susie Burmann, who has made a business out of seeing the beauty that others miss.

Susie knows her antiques as well as she knows her Midwest, an education that first came to her by way of her mother. "My mother furnished our farmhouse with antiques when I was growing up, out of necessity," she relates, "not as a collector. It was before collecting was fashionable."

The farm was a shorthorn cattle operation in Marion, Indiana, and Susie was a full-fledged farmhand. "I loved the hard work and the work ethic it left me with," she says. She also loved the farm animals. "I was

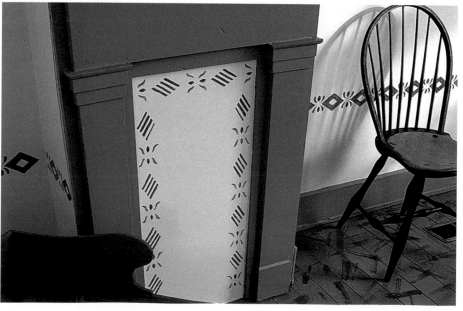

ABOVE: Using "fine forms of country furniture in as original condition as possible," the Burmanns have developed a collection that looks as though it has been in place since 1830, when the dwelling was built.
LEFT: Stenciling on the fireplace insert echoes, but does not match, the walls in a house that revels in a variety of patterns.

very active in the 4-H club for ten years. One year I won the award for top showman in the whole state." She adds, proudly, "That was quite an achievement for a girl back then!"

Marriage to Rich Burmann brought her to West Point, New York, where her husband was a physical education instructor at the U.S. Military Academy. Susie taught school. The couple lived in a handsome carriage house on the former estate of the financier, J. P. Morgan.

Hudson River Valley auctions provided cheap Friday night entertainment for the Burmanns and whetted their appetite for antiques. Auctions place a mirror to a region, revealing its decorative arts and traditions.

"We made a lot of mistakes, buying things at those auctions," Susie recalls, "but the experience got us on the right track, as far as antiques go. It gave us a better understanding of what furnishings were appropriate for the house that we were living in. And it encouraged us to

start studying the field, to learn more."

When they finally returned to the Midwest, continuing in their teaching careers, the Burmanns began looking for a house that would be suitable for the Early American furniture they had collected over the years.

"The focus of our collection was fine country pieces, mostly 18th- and 19th-century, with emphasis on pieces in their original condition, or very close," Susie says. "And, we liked to buy only furniture that we would actually use in our home."

At the same time, the couple was developing the inventory that would form the core of their antiques business. A slant-top desk they purchased at an antiques shop in Indiana set the tone for this business. "It was cherry, with a French foot, 18th-century, and probably made in Pennsylvania," says Susie. "It was a quality piece, the first thing of any serious nature that we obtained."

After five years of searching for their ideal residence, the couple finally located a house that was large enough to serve both as their private home and a place for their budding enterprise.

"The Judge's Town House," as it was known—because four generations of a

LEFT: Treasured examples of paint-decorated antiques include an early-19th-century blanket chest with original painted surface and smoke decoration, and an elaborate New England dome-top box with original paint.
ABOVE: Some 12,000 antique bricks were hand-cleaned by the owners in the course of their house's restoration.

jurist's family had lived there—was a twenty-three-room townhouse built in the 1830s. It had plenty of character, but plenty of problems, too.

"The first year we lived in the house, its condition was so bad," Susie recalls with bemusement. "The only lighting came from a string of patio lights strung up in the house. The only running water was in an upstairs bathtub. There was only one working toilet, downstairs. The kitchen was nonexistent." Friends of the Burmanns tried to be encouraging of the couple's renovation project. "But they told me later that they would go home from a visit here in tears, so overwhelmed by what lay ahead for us!"

Richard and Susie literally rolled up their sleeves. "Things that required no skill, such as cleaning twelve thousand bricks, we did ourselves," relates Susie, who quit her teaching job to manage the project and the creative financing it required. "When an estimate came in, we'd just sell another antique to raise the money."

Common sense helped them make the right decisions during what really was a full-scale historic restoration project. "We let the house tell its own story, and we learned to listen," she says. "The simplest answers always turned out to be the best."

Moving in, the Burmanns were determined to enliven the house with a style that fitted its period, but with 20th-century livability.

"I tried to get into the minds of the original dwellers, but not to live in their era," Susie says, as she went about the job of furnishing the house with antiques. A 19th-century American cupboard did the job of standard storage cabinets in the kitchen. Hoop-back Windsor chairs and a stretcher-base table with original green paint found places elsewhere. Quilts, linsey woolsey coverlets, and an old serape rug added their flourishes.

A mint-condition Pennsylvania sampler that reads, "Susana Watson. 1809" is not for sale (Watson is Susie's maiden name), but almost everything else is. "Now we live with our inventory," says Susie, "which means sometimes we do without a kitchen table" that a customer has taken. But the Burmanns don't rush out to buy a new one. "We just wait until something better comes along."

ABOVE: A homemade box wears its heart on its chip-carved top. BELOW: Painted urns carry over a classical motif from the "found" mantel to the newly treated walls. The designs are variations on 19th-century stencil patterns, reproduced here by artist Barbara Gephart in collaboration with the owners. OPPOSITE: Early paint colors and textiles give the upstairs quarters a strong period flavor. In the far bedroom, the monogrammed bed skirt, made in 1910, belonged to Richard Burmann's grandmother. The cradle in the foreground with its elaborate gold-leaf decoration is stamped with its original label, dated 1870.

the allure of painted Furniture

Paints, dyes, and other artifices were used from the earliest days of Colonial America to embellish walls, floors,

furniture, and other household objects. The high prices that many of the antiques from this period command today belie their relatively humble histories. For example, a lot of pine furniture was painted with trompe l'oeil whorls and grains so that it resembled the more expensive hardwood chairs, tables, and chests of the upper class. And stenciling was invented in those early days to simulate the high-priced imported wallpaper that only the wealthiest families could afford to have.

So what we regard today as exquisite examples of the decorative arts were really only efforts to dissemble.

Painted furniture has a long, honorable tradition. In Europe it was found in the rustic farmhouses and country estates of the hinterlands, and the sophisticated city apartments and royal palaces of the most privileged classes of the realms.

History carried the art of decorating furniture to European shores. During the Napoleonic Wars, the French discovered Egypt's tradition of painting wood surfaces, which dates back to the time of the Pharoahs. Even more influential was the opening to the Orient and the discovery of the technique of lacquering wood surfaces as practiced in China and Japan. Eventually, lacquering became known as "japanning."

Once the basic idea of decorating wood surfaces was imported from the East, European craftsmen did not take long to adapt the techniques in their own singular ways. Glazing and coloring wood surfaces became an art form unto itself in the Renaissance countries of France and Italy. English cabinetmakers copied Oriental lacquers by using varnishes and pigments. Meanwhile, in central and eastern Europe, German and Slav peoples used visual motifs that came out of the Middle Ages and the Renaissance to give their painted furniture its unique stamp.

Many of these traditions devolved into the furniture crafted and embellished in the New World. In the Massachusetts Bay Colony of the 1650s, wood surfaces were decorated in floral motifs with oil paints.

Perhaps no early Americans excelled at the art of painting furniture more than the Pennsylvania Dutch—German-speaking people who settled in Pennsylvania in droves from 1750 to 1850 (the "Dutch" here is an Americanization of *Deutsch*). They felt compelled to decorate the objects of their daily life—chests and boxes, pottery, glassware, and rugs—with their favorite floral and avian themes.

Even the simplest painted furniture reveals the hand of a proud owner.

An Eye for
Choosing the Best

I T'S ONE THING TO WORK THE antiques circuit of a Sunday, checking out the local flea markets, antiques fairs, and emporia at a leisurely pace. It's another to be constantly on the road, always setting up, packing up, moving on to the next stop on the show circuit. But that's a dealer's lot.

"Both the best and worst part about this business is the travel," says Adrian Cote, a clinical psychologist who gave up his practice to join his wife, Judith George, in the trade.

Judith apprenticed early in the world of antiquing. She was just a teenager when her older brother started taking her with him to auctions and estate sales. "I became interested in vintage clothing and jewelry, and by eighteen, I had my own business," she says.

It took Judith years to coax and cajole Adrian into the business with her. The breakthrough came when the couple decided to use a move from Connecticut to South Bend, Indiana, Judith's hometown, as an excuse to travel extensively.

The restored backgrounds of this 1920s Spanish colonial dwelling showcase a dealer's impressive collection of 19th- and early-20th-century Native American artifacts, including Navajo Eyedazzler rugs and Cherokee river cane baskets. OPPOSITE: A carved wood weathervane from a centennial farmhouse makes an intriguing silhouette in a quiet stairwell.

For a year, they drove the byways of North America, poking in shops and stores, visiting galleries and museums, observing the antiques and collectibles that were unique for each region. When they made several stops at Indian reservations, Adrian found himself back in touch with a special interest that had made a powerful impression on him as a student.

"While at the University of Colorado, I became enthralled with Native American culture," he recalls. "The school museum had an excellent curator, Joe Ben Wheat, and he arranged for frequent exhibitions of Native American art. I loved the work and felt an emotional bond with the peoples who had produced it. Little did I know that I'd be selling their stuff now!"

In South Bend, the couple settled into a house in one of the town's oldest histori-cal neighborhoods—a house that looks as if it were moved here from Southern California or the Southwest. "Our house was one of many built here during the 1920s, when industrial growth brought affluence to the Midwest," Judith explains. "Typically, people of that time would be capti-vated by residential styles they saw on their travels east or out west. Then they'd return to South Bend and have houses like that built, even using materials and craftsmen from outside the region."

Restoration of the house interiors left ample white-walled spaces to showcase the antiques the couple began to amass, working as a team in the field for the first time. The house fairly radiates with their collections of 19th-century Eyedazzler Navajo blankets, 19th-century Ameri-can furniture, and early-20th-century

LEFT: A Maine sea chest, handpainted with bucolic scenes to remind an earlier traveler of home, is anchored in a sea of black ash splint and seagrass baskets, made by Penobscot Indians for the 1880s tourist trade. OPPOSITE: In a Hoosier dining room, the Wild West is celebrated in a sweeping panorama (found in a Michigan tavern and signed "P. Hutchings, 1950") that shares wall space with an 1860 Georgia hunt board, which has an unusual pair of top-mounted knife boxes.

Cherokee Indian river cane baskets.

Now fully committed to the working life of a dealer, and its working philosophy, Adrian takes the view that "everything's for sale, including the house," explaining, "if you're in this business and you're honest, you can't hold back your best material or your favorite pieces. You really have to offer your customers the best of what you find. Whether someone is spending $100 or $10,000, nobody wants second best."

A Maine native, Adrian has a special fondness for the collection of Penobscot Indian baskets he and Judith have assembled. "They're not rare or expensive—$50 to $150—and you can still find examples that are a hundred years old," says Adrian. "There's no 'show appeal' for them, yet they hold a lot of appeal for us and they are fun to find."

Adrian believes that "pristine condition" is not necessarily the sine qua non of a great antique. "I found a Navajo serape that was in terrible condition, 90 percent threadbare," he explains. "But its style was so outstanding, that didn't matter. It showed its age, but it also showed its incredible beauty. So even a beat-up piece can be the best of its kind."

He also has learned what Judith understood from the beginning, that knowledge is what separates the good dealer from the wheeler dealer.

"You have to know about quality and what makes one piece unique and another just ordinary," he asserts. "If I have a hundred Navajo rugs, there will be one that stands out. It takes a knowing eye to find that, but that's why good dealers stay in business. Their clients trust and respect their judgment, and come back for more."

Finding the diamond in the rough, then finding the customer for the diamond, is what dealing in fine antiques is all about.

TOP: The feather detailing on a Maine chest of drawers, dating from 1840, and on the box on top, was commissioned to create the impression of a richer wood such as mahogany. A collection of basswood and birchbark trinkets attests to the artistry of the Minnesota Ojibwa Indians, while the profile of the brave comes from the talents of an unknown Illinois artist. ABOVE: A painted chest of drawers epitomizes Victorian cottage style. OPPOSITE: Period columned arches and ironwork are original architectural elements preserved by extensive renovation of a historic property.

the art of **Picking**

It is a job as essential to the antiques trade as scouting is to major league baseball, but few even know of its existence.  It's the job of "picker," the roving collector who buys not for himself but for his network of dealers. Like the baseball scout, the picker knows what he's looking at, and what he's looking for.

"I'm just a curious person by nature," says picker Robert Zollinhofer. "I'm not trained in history or architecture, but I've learned by looking and studying. This firsthand knowledge is called experience." Shrewdly, Robert will canvas specialty shows, not for the goods that are there in volume, but for the odd object from another time or style. "From a 1950s show, I bought an early country piece for a price that would have been much higher at a show devoted to country," he notes. "At a country show, I came upon a fine, formal mirror, again something available at a good price because there were no takers. I was in the right place at the right time." Pickers also haunt flea markets, estate sales, yard sales, consignment shops, thrift shops, bankruptcy sales, and any other locale where an antique or collectible may be found "for the picking" at below wholesale or better. They are not averse to knocking on a stranger's door to inquire, "Anything you might want to clear out of your attic today?"

Some pickers occupy highly specialized niches. Ralph Lauren has turned to pickers who trade exclusively in Western cowboy memorabilia, English country relics, American folk art, or old sporting gear, which he buys from them to create an authentic, steeped-in-time character in his retail stores. Other pickers are generalists who travel from town to town looking on behalf of a variety of dealers, each with different tastes and needs. They pride themselves on knowing what kind of merchandise their clients seek, and what they will pay for it. They might come home from a weekend in the country with a van or station wagon loaded with quilts for one customer, garden ornaments for another, and china for a third.

Even more so than ardent collectors, pickers go about their business with an unbridled enthusiasm for sniffing out the treasures buried in the heaps of things stashed in a garage or the back of a secondhand shop. They have cultivated a sharp eye for the standout object and a great instinct for the current demands of an ever-changing market. As much as they delight in the quest, they are not about to pay more for something than they should, and they wrangle for the best possible price. Then, as the coldhearted businesspeople they must be, they part with their finds without a qualm. Generally, the picker looks for a profit of about 25 percent when he is able to turn goods over rapidly. Because the picker leads a gypsy existence, he can afford to operate on a slim margin and, by selling quickly, is free to reinvest. The dealer, shouldering overhead and other expenses, needs to average a profit of 100 percent on sales in order to stay in business.

A Loyal Clientele

AN OBVIOUS BUT OFTEN overlooked quality in an antiques dealer is the capacity for handling the public. The best dealers are those who take genuine pleasure in people, and in helping them derive more pleasure from the antiques they buy for their home. By those standards, Barbara Doherty ranks near the top. Pineapple Primitives, the shop she opened first in Brooklyn Heights, then at the South Street Seaport in New York, became a magnet for collectors who valued Barbara not only for what she sold but for who she is.

Her trend-setting shop in the Brooklyn storefront was exciting to visit. "People out for their nightly walks made detours to be sure they passed the corner of Hicks and Pineapple Streets," Barbara remembers. "I had big windows to work with and there was always great curiosity to see 'what Barbara has in her window now.'" In the 1960s and 1970s, the furniture called "golden oak" was the affordable antique of

A mural painted in 1916 by Mildred Burridge, a Maine artist who studied under Monet, depicts familiar Kennebunkport landmarks which survive to this day, including the columned Knott mansion, home to the local historical society. Shaker boxes sit on an 18th-century American tavern table with scrub top and original paint. OPPOSITE: The entry of a Maine house dating from 1775, dressed for the season, has its original wide-plank pine floorboards with square nails.

choice, but Barbara preferred to display older, more enduring rustic pieces from the 18th and 19th century. "I've always been attracted to primitive things," Barbara says. She was one of the first dealers to recognize the value and appeal of quilts, decoys, baskets, redware, crocks, blue-and-white Cantonware, and such innovations as weathervanes as ornaments for the house.

"The customers are what kept me going in business," says Barbara, who now lives in Kennebunkport, Maine. Not long ago, she was invited to a house along the Hudson River for lunch. The homeowner immediately recognized her, Barbara relates. "She said, 'Why, I bought an Indian basket from you years and years ago. You had it displayed on top of a cupboard. I still have it, and I still love it!'" That, says Barbara, is why she found dealing in antiques so rewarding. "It's gratifying to place something that had great beauty in a house where it will be appreciated for a long time," she explains.

Barbara did not set out to be a dealer, but she always loved merchandising. She worked as a wedding consultant for B. Altman after marrying and coming to New York from her native Ohio. Her family and later job in a Manhattan search firm occupied her fully during the 1960s. "I always had an eye for accessories," she says, "finding new uses for old things, but I pretty much limited that

talent to decorating my own house."

In the thirty-some years that Barbara has been dealing in antiques, she has always stuck by her own tastes. "Your eye becomes more sophisticated with time," she observes. "It's the same thing that makes a personal wardrobe come together. You learn to edit your antiques the way you edit your clothes, until you arrive at the best—those objects or pieces of furniture that stand out."

Maine, where Barbara gathered so many of the antique pieces that filled her shops, now provides a congenial home, itself full of history. Her house, Tory Chimneys, is actually three, possibly four, residences in one, with a total of seven fireplaces. One ell is the original one-room house built about 1740 by Benjamin Coes, a sailmaker from Marblehead, Massachusetts, who used the loft above for his sailmaking business. In one wing of the house, murals painted in 1916 depict early Kennebunkport scenes.

Barbara lives today with the antiques she most cherishes. "I think I may be pretty well satisfied after all these years in the business," she says. "The things in my house are right for their period and right for this sort of house," from an 18th-century New Hampshire stepback cupboard with original blue paint, to an early American rocking horse—the very first primitive art she collected as a teenager back in Ohio.

ABOVE: In the mural room, graceful antique furniture forms are accentuated by new slipcovers, while others are appreciated on their own merits. Dried hydrangeas in a cast-iron cemetery urn complement the Queen Anne tiger-maple tea table. RIGHT: A time capsule of artifacts found under attic floorboards during a renovation of the house included a letter from the original builder, Benjamin Coes, to his brother Samuel, and a piece of sailcloth dating from the 18th century, when the attic was used as a sailmaker's loft. OPPOSITE, ABOVE: A Scottish country Windsor chair and a French hanging cupboard lend warmth to a master bathroom complete with original hearth. Potted myrtle topiaries, grown locally at Snug Harbor Farm, and old Long Island shorebird carvings add their unique forms to the setting. OPPOSITE, BELOW: In another corner of the mural room a painted folk-art horse adds a welcome dose of whimsy.

The dining room is a tribute to 18th-century craftsmanship, with its cherry table bench, banister-back New England side chairs, and blanket chest with original paint. The primitive rocking horse with horsehair mane and tail was the first collectible Barbara Doherty ever acquired.

The Beauty of
Original Details

I T'S ALL IN THE WOOD," DECLARES
dealer/picker Robert Zollinhofer,
explaining why he examines
scrubbed tops, crackled spirit-
varnish treatments, and original second finishes of antique furniture with
the scrutiny of a detective. "Wood
tells you the age of a piece, its origin,
and just about everything else," says
the former Cornell University profes-
sor of biology, who now applies the
laws of science to his quest for the
best of authentic Early American
furnishings.

Robert examines furniture for its
tool marks, pigments and gradations
of color, surface condition and condition of the blocks used in its construction, the shrinkage time has
imposed on it, and whether any or all
of it has been repaired, replaced,
restored, or refinished. Oil or waxed
surfaces do not appeal to Robert. "I
like a 'dry' surface—one that has
remained unaltered over time," he
says. "It does a lot for the value of an
antique and appeals to a better collector, who will pay a premium for it."

Taking "unaltered" to the max is

A holdover from the dwelling's past existence as an inn, the ballroom is furnished with the styles of the times, including mid-18th-century Hudson Valley shoefoot hutch tables, New England Queen Anne maple chairs made in 1750, an 18th-century New England wigstand, and a deck of playing cards from 1834. OPPOSITE: In the upstairs landing room of this early-18th-century Ohio homestead, a 1790 birchwood tall chest from Portsmouth, New Hampshire, is brightened by a dome-top small chest with original 1740 needlepoint covering.

best exemplified in the antique house Robert painstakingly restored over a two-year period to look like "one of the old abandoned houses you'd find in a wheat field up here." Situated on its original site in Medina, Ohio, the wood-sheathed dwelling was built in 1818 by a young New Englander who came with a second wave of settlers to the Western Reserve in northern Ohio.

"One hundred acres of land was deeded to military men of rank to settle this area after the Revolutionary War," explains Robert. Most of the houses built in Ohio at this time reflected the Greek Revival style of the day. "Thomas Jefferson was President and the house plans of his architect, Asher Benjamin, were widely circulated," he adds. "They got into the hands of just about every housewright in the country."

However, Robert's house differed from the columned facades that prevailed at the time, because its original builder fol-

lowed his own lights. "Burritt Blakeslee came to Ohio from Connecticut when he was just sixteen. He built this house in the style that he knew best, using pre–Revolutionary Connecticut timber-frame construction." According to records, the house took about four years to complete. Blakeslee made his own tools and set up a sawmill to supply the sheathing for interior and exterior walls, millwork and floors. Timber was plentiful in this region, and green oak harvested off the property was used for the mortise-and-tenon joinery to support the hand-hewn frame. Only window glass and iron for making nails had to be brought in from afar, arriving by wagon train.

The homestead has remained intact through nearly two centuries because of its peculiar history. At first, situated on a major thoroughfare to the West, it functioned as an inn, as the seat of local government, and as a social center for the community. "But, as the area became more settled," says Robert, "the house fell out of fashion and the original owners fell on hard times."

Robert discovered the house in a state of limbo, never modernized, still with all its original detailing—his favorite kind of wood. "The old, undisturbed surface finishes and paint are what give the house its character and importance," he says. It has become the ideal receptacle for the dealer's stellar collection of early country and early Federal antiques. "I wanted to keep the house just as the original family had lived in it, with pre–Revolutionary furniture," such as the Pilgrim chest, shoe-foot hutch table, and banister-back chairs in the keeping room, the pencil-post bed in the bedroom, the formal mahogany in the dining room, and the English pewter candlesticks in the parlor.

SUNDAY	MONDAY	TUESDAY	WEDNESDAY	THURSDAY
dim dom son	lun lun mon	mar mar die	mer miér mit	jeu jue don

APRIL 2002
	1	2	3	4	5	6
7	8	9	10	11	12	13
14	15	16	17	18	19	20
21	22	23	24	25	26	27
28	29	30

JUNE 2002
						1
2	3	4	5	6	7	8
9	10	11	12	13	14	15
16	17	18	19	20	21	22
23	24	25	26	27	28	29
30

1
May Day
Fête du Travail (FRANCE)
Día del Trabajo (MÉXICO)
Workers' Day (SOUTH AFRICA)

2

5
Batalla de Puebla (MÉXICO)
Children's Day (JAPAN)
こどもの日

6
Bank Holiday (U.K., IRELAND)
May Day
(NORTHERN TERRITORY, AU)
Labour Day (QUEENSLAND, AU)

7

8
Fête de la Victoire (FRANCE)

9

NEW ● MOON
10:46 U.T.
Dave Matthews Concert
12
Mother's Day (U.S., CANADA,
AUSTRALIA, NEW ZEALAND)

13

14

15

16

1ST ☽ QTR
19:43 U.T.
19
Pentecost
Pentecôte
Pentecostés

20
Victoria Day (CANADA)

21

22

23

FULL ○ MOON
11:52 U.T.
26
Trinity Sunday
Domingo de la Santa Trinidad
Vesak (BIRTH & ENLIGHTENMENT
OF BUDDHA)

27
Memorial Day (U.S., OBSERVED)
Bank Holiday (U.K.)

28

29

30
Corpus Christi

ABOVE: Original to the room, the 1835 hand-printed French wallpaper was preserved in places where it had deteriorated by painstakingly matching color photocopies of the floral pattern to the antique paper. On an 18th-century Pembroke table is a carved ivory chess set made in 1800 by prisoners during the Napoleonic Wars and used to trade for food. In spite of English repugnance for the emperor, toby mugs made in his likeness were popular collectibles. RIGHT: The bar is still open in the ballroom; in an earlier age, the term referred not to the counter, but the wooden bars used to secure the liquor stock when it was left unattended. FAR RIGHT: Never modernized, the house retains its original detailing, including the grain-painted mustard yellow stairs, floors, and walls of the upstairs landing. OPPOSITE: The bird's-eye maple Sheraton youth bed, made on Boston's north shore, is topped with a canopy with lace from nearby Ipswich, Massachusetts.

Midwestern turn-of-the-century impresssions of the Wild West are found in an Indiana cigar store figure and the Ohio hooked rug bought at a flea market. On the mantel is a 1940 Mickey Mouse alarm clock; hung below a Pennsylvania-made "Kentucky" rifle with silver inlay in the shape of fish—"More of these rifles were made in Pennsylvania than in Kentucky," notes Robert. OPPOSITE: In one bedroom, the grandfather clock, with comb-painted surface and seven different colors, was exhibited at the World's Fair in Tumbridge, Vermont, in 1806. A rarity, it was assembled from 1,000 sets of clockworks and faces made by the best clockmakers in the Connecticut River Valley as a special commission for the Porter Contract Works of Tumbridge.

Robert's love for antiques began when he was in college. "I brought a Model A Ford right off the farm with me to school. It was cheap and it ran. The fenders had been patched and held together with baling wire. After college I decided to sell it," he explains. "I put a 'For Sale' sign on it at a car show that I unwittingly entered. When it won the 'booby prize,' I got on the mike and announced that here I was looking out at a sea of so-called antique cars. But all I could see was a lot of new rubber, new paint, and new fenders. There was only one authentic antique in the field, I said, and it was mine!"

To Robert, the beauty is in being original. Like all those vintage autos passing for antiques, furniture is susceptible to misrepresentation. "I would buy a gateleg table with a replaced drawer, but I would not buy one with a 'married' top," he explains. (In the antiques trade, "marriage" is a term meaning the combination of originally unrelated but compatible parts to make one complete piece of furniture.) The original top distinguishes the piece. "Every good dealer I know has a gateleg table base sitting in their attic. One day, I'm going to find an original top," and watch the research pay off. "I'll run an advertisement in the trades," he muses. "I bet I get a hundred calls!"

the romance of Wood

"When the first Europeans came to our shores," writes Donald Culross Peattie, the poet laureate of North American tree flora, "our virgin forests, stretching from ocean to ocean and from arctic strand to tropic, staggered the belief . . . First the trees were barriers and ambushes, then they became blockhouses and cabins, gunstocks and cradles, wagon wheels and railway ties." The forests then were the grandest and most varied of all the earth's temperate zones, and they became the building blocks of the New World—and multitudes of houses, and furniture of every description, as native woods were harvested to literally build and shape the American way of life.

Hardwoods come from broadleaf trees, like ash, cherry, beech, hickory, maple, oak, and walnut. They have durable surfaces, not easily dented or damaged, and rich, complex grain patterns. When furniture is to remain unpainted and uncovered, it is usually made with wood from the hardwood family. Hardwoods are used for most veneers as well.

Softwoods come from needle-bearing trees like pine, poplar, redwood, spruce, fir, and cedar. They are physically softer than hardwoods (although there are some exceptions, such as pitch pine and yew, both of which are almost as hard as oak) and can be easily nicked. Less costly than hardwoods, they are often used in rustic and other vernacular furniture styles, and as secondary woods in pieces to be covered with hardwoods. Many softwoods are used in marquetry because they absorb stains beautifully.

The Windsor chair, the quintessential country seat in America, is an amalgam of hardwoods and softwoods. Chestnut, hickory, oak, or ash are used to make the chair's bent elements. Pine or tulip poplar go into the seat. Maple, chestnut, oak, or hickory are used for all turned parts. If nothing else, this explains the difficulty dealers and collectors sometimes have in establishing exactly what kind of wood is in the furniture that comes into their hands.

Some of America's most storied woods are:

WHITE ASH—a strong, light, flexible hardwood used in bentwood chairs, garden tools, porch furniture, oars and keels of small boats, and baseball boats.

WILD BLACK CHERRY—one of our finest cabinet woods, noted for its smooth grain, hard finish, ability to take a handsome finish, and refusal to warp after seasoning, no matter what changes occur in temperature or moisture.

HICKORY—wood from the school of hard knocks, able to withstand rough treatment in all kinds of weather, used extensively in Adirondack camp furniture, often with the bark left on. Early furniture makers used seasoned rounds of shagbark hickory in posts of green maple to create unbreakable joinery—"As the green wood shrank," writes Peattie, "it clasped the iron-hard hickory dowels forever."

SUGAR MAPLE (OR ROCK MAPLE)—in demand for furniture since the earliest cabinetmakers of New England plied their trade. The immensely strong sapwood in maple has outlasted marble as flooring, and fancy bird's-eye maple grains have graced many a bedroom set.

EASTERN WHITE OAK—considered the best all-purpose wood of the American hardwood family, and used by the pioneers for two centuries for their log cabins, barns, bridges, and mills. In the "golden Oak era" of early 1900s, it became the vogue among nouveaux riches to panel entire rooms with ostentatiously varnished, machine-cut oak panels; today, it is often used for flooring and ornamental veneers.

WHITE PINE—possibly the most useful tree of all, found in the paneling of fine old Colonial interiors, the sleighs and bobsleds of New England, the shingles, window sashes, and doors of millions of frame houses, and untold numbers of country cupboards, chairs, and tables.

BLACK WALNUT—before becoming scarce, provided the finest cabinet wood of North America, used extensively in homemade furniture of the Colonial and Federal periods, and even exported to England for the same purpose as early as 1610. Today, walnut is grown chiefly for its handsome and varied grain and used as elegant veneer.

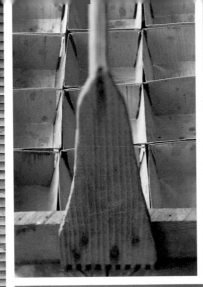

A House
Like No One Else's

N THE WORLD OF DEALERS, there's more than one way to fill a barn. Nashville dealer Joy Haley parked a bumper pool table in the barn of the family's country house and covered the walls with a useful collection of mismatched ladderback chairs, unified by coats of white paint. "I can't pass up an old country chair," she says. "They're cheap, charming, and you can never have enough of them if you entertain in large groups the way we do." She hung dozens of them from nails to free up floor space for storing farm equipment and her latest antiques finds.

Her penchant for collecting old things was passed down to her by her mother. "I would go out antiquing with my mother when I was a child," Joy recalls. "I loved it all—the looking, the finding, and asking all kinds of questions. Mother would invariably come home with something a little unorthodox or a tad different, from a shop or an auction. She recognized the decorative value of architectural elements long

Slipcovered to empha-
size their classic forms,
upholstered pieces are
used to furnish the
country house of dealer
Joy Haley. Canines—
painted, carved, and
needlepointed—have
been given the run of
the place. OPPOSITE:
The relaxed spirit of
Idlewild is evoked in the
playfulness of a new
Federal-style mirror
paired with an antique
English demilune
mahogany table.

Muslin-draped interiors of the past are recalled in the parlor, where furnishings and windows are covered in a combination of crewel, duck, and linen fabrics. The collection of 19th-century antiques includes an Empire secretary as old as the house. OPPOSITE, ABOVE: Antiques earn their keep in a summer kitchen as supplemental work surfaces, extra seating, and wall decoration.

before people started hanging them on walls. She had a fun way with things."

Even as a girl, Joy was attracted to the style of the old farmhouses found in the rural countryside of southwestern Kentucky. "My dad had a Ford dealership, and I would ride around in the county with him making truck deliveries," she says. One house, a brick Greek Revival dwelling built in the 1830s, made a powerful impression on her when she was a teenager. It was called "Idlewild" and it seemed to her the perfect place to live.

As a young bride, Joy would make her husband, Bob, drive them past Idlewild whenever they came home from Vanderbilt University in Nashville, where he was still a student. "I'd make him turn off the highway, just so I could go past the house one more time," she laughs. Then, in 1984, the house went on the auction block. The Haleys put in a bid. Next thing they knew, they were the proud owners. The house needed extensive repairs and renovation she notes, "but the 'bones' were already there and this made it easy to preserve its structural integrity."

Joy furnished Idlewild with antiques,

The owner places a premium on old things that still serve practical needs, from beverage crocks to country furniture. Her 14-foot table, with scrub top and painted base, once functioned as an old store counter.

but avoided slavishly copying a period theme that would have been inappropriate and impractical for a second residence. To soften rooms, she slipcovered old upholstered frames in cotton duck and crewelwork in a range of cream colors. A secretary of about the same vintage as the house took up a commanding position in the living room. Her collections bring life to the rooms. "I didn't set out to collect dog things," she notes, "but I have a lot of paintings and pieces of needlework with dogs on them. My daddy hunted with dogs and I grew up with them as pets, so I wasn't surprised to find that a collection had materialized under my nose."

Other collections formed in the same

TOP: The lazy Susan table, the dining room's centerpiece, was found at an estate sale. Surrounding it are ladderback chairs from Joy Haley's mother and "porch Windsors" dressed in their own slipcovers. The Kentucky walnut corner cupboard and old portrait of sporting dogs are both flea market finds. ABOVE: Idlewild remained in the same family from 1843 to 1985, when the Haleys bought it at auction.

Vintage rocking horses add their sprightly presence to the boys' bedroom, along with an old poplar wardrobe with faded red paint, new wicker bedsteads by Ralph Lauren, and relics of the sporting life (including a bowl filled with old painted croquet balls that Joy Haley has been collecting for twenty years).

way. "I have so many old baskets because I use them for just about everything," she explains, from bringing tomatoes in from the garden, or gathering wildflowers across the road, to carting puppies to the vet. For Joy, things have to be useful, not just beautiful. "I love my old silver and I use it everyday," she says. "I use my antique quilts—we sleep under them and the boys grew up sleeping under them. I don't use paper napkins. I use my old linen napkins. I don't have collections of anything that can't be used."

Like her mother before her, Joy has become adept at bringing home surprises. Visitors acknowledge that her original eye has made Idlewild a special place. One day one of her sons asked, "Mom, what's wrong with our house?"

"Nothing. Why do you ask?" Joy replied.

"Well," he told his mother, "a friend of mine said, 'You know, your house doesn't look like anybody else's.'"

"I took it as a compliment!" Joy declares.

ABOVE LEFT: The Victorian portrait of children holding toys, above an early-19th-century English oak chest, was found at a flea market. ABOVE: An imposing Empire bed, another auction prize, lends gravity to an ordinary bedroom. BELOW LEFT: Period fixtures like the flea market pedestal sink supply the house with modern plumbing convenience.

Dealer's Country

LIKE SO MANY ANTIQUES dealers, Marge has nurtured a passion born of necessity. "I started going to country auctions to furnish our first home. It was a turn-of-the-century farmhouse with oak paneling that reminded me of an English cottage. My husband Al and I wanted to fill it with things that were appropriate," the dealer explains. An oak commode for $30 was her first acquisition, far removed from the early-18th-century furnishings that fill their house today.

When beginning, most dealers don't have the luxury of holding on to the rare or the first-rate for very long. By assiduously trading up, they can improve their fortunes over the years to the point where they, too, can afford the collector's indulgence of keeping the things they cherish.

Now 18th-century New England pieces, along with early Ohio-made furniture (in original paint), circa 1830, have become Marge's stock-in-trade. "I started out buying things that I loved and, as I could afford to, I'd upgrade for quality, buying earlier and earlier pieces. If I had my way,"

Vintage decorated stoneware and New England painted pantry boxes line the shelves of the buttery where butter- and cheese-making containers were originally stored. OPPOSITE: The period cupboard in the keeping room was relocated from a nearby house of the same era and slightly altered to fit the space. The early banister-back chair from Massachusetts is dated 1730.

BELOW: The oval shoefoot hutch table, circa 1710, was made in New England; the large woodenware Pease sugar container on top comes from Ohio. BOTTOM: Crewelwork curtains that once graced the home of Indiana author Booth Tarkington add a decorative note to a room dominated by a 1760 Connecticut maple high chest, spared the addition of decorative hardware down through the years. OPPOSITEE: Antiques from the early 18th century, infusing a bedroom with New England character, include a 1730 Connecticut blanket chest with paint decoration and a linsey-woolsey quilted spread.

she adds, "it would all be 18th century."

As a child growing up in the country, Marge was fascinated by the many old houses that dotted the rolling landscape around Medina County, which is located in the Western Reserve of northern Ohio. "I've always loved old houses, probably because I was raised in one," she says, recalling the joys of poking around cubbyholes, exploring the attic eaves, and playing in the summer kitchen of her family's 1860 farmhouse. She and her husband had always dreamed of owning a period house, but Ohio houses weren't early enough for them. "There are a few center-chimney houses in Ohio, but they are circa 1800." So determined were they to live in an early-18th-century house that they contemplated moving to New England. Instead, they moved New England to them.

The center-chimney colonial that now sits high on a hilltop overlooking a lush valley of pastureland and trees was built by Isaac King in 1712 in Plympton, Massachusetts. The historic dwelling was disassembled and carted to its present site in Ohio in 1975.

It took eighteen months for the couple, who acted as contractors on the job, to reconstruct the 264-year-old dwelling. "When the Massachusetts crew left, after

ABOVE: The center chimney colonial was built in 1712 by Isaac King in Plympton, Massachusetts, then moved and reconstructed on its present site near the Western Reserve of Ohio in 1975.

A collection of furniture with original red paint is shown off to advantage against the red walls of the keeping room. Ladderback chairs with untouched surfaces surround a scrub-top table, circa 1780, with sawbuck base. Its centerpiece is an Indian-made burl bowl with red paint. Positioned near the hearth is an early Massachusetts settle, also with original paint, whose high back and winged sides helped collect heat from the hearth, drawing people "to settle in" the space.

reassembling the dismantled frame, we were pretty much on our own. We had no written manual to turn to," Marge explains. One of their challenges was getting the Ohio crew to leave well enough alone. "They kept wanting to straighten the old walls and floors, and we wanted them left the way they had always been—crooked," she recalls.

Furnishing the house with antiques of the period posed an enjoyable challenge. "The minute I knew we were buying this house, I started acquiring furniture of that period. We had some pieces in the other house that I thought I'd never want

to sell—fine pieces from Pennsylvania and Ohio. Funny how past treasures lose their character in the wrong surroundings."

With few exceptions, the house is now furnished with pieces the original Isaac King family might have owned—New England (mostly Massachusetts) antiques with original surfaces or original paint, dating from as early as 1710 to about 1780.

When the site was being excavated for the house, the couple found a cache of Indian arrowheads. "I love the country," Marge adds, "the farms, the open land, all nature," and, she is quick to point out, "the earliest antiques I can find!"

shopping for Antiques

Here are some strategies for successful antiquing in the most popular venues of the trade.

ANTIQUES SHOPS. These range from general-line small-town emporia to specialized—and expensive—haute antique purveyors found at better addresses in the big cities. High-end shops that specialize in periods or categories of furniture are run by dealers who know their stuff. Some collectors are more likely to experience the thrill of the hunt in shops that carry a large jumble of inventory, typically lots of small household goods—textiles, tools, glassware and china—mixed with furniture, toys and dolls, jewelry, books, sporting items, lamps, quilts, rugs, and primitives. True, there are treasures to be found in these shops, but often much of the merchandise is of only modest importance or value, and may not even qualify as antique. Furthermore, the intrepid shopper may know as much, if not more, about a certain treasure than the shop owner, who cannot possibly keep up with every field represented by the eclectic offerings.

ESTATE SALES. Tag sales and garage sales, designed to empty the unwanted contents of somebody's attic, basement, or garage, rarely yield much of value to the collector. Estate sales, however, are worth a detour, for they dispose of the possessions a family actually lived with over several generations. Dealers eager for inventory are in abundance at these events, too, so it is important to be focused when perusing the merchandise, and decisive when you see something you like. When estate sales are held over a two- or three-day period, as is customary, you may be able to negotiate better prices for things toward the end of the sale period—if you're willing to risk the things being bought by other collectors for the asking price.

ANTIQUES SHOWS AND MARKETS. These events are worth the price of admission—and they do charge admission—if only because the merchandise on exhibit is all either old or highly collectible. These are good places to pursue an education in antiques. Prices are high, but the dealers are all knowledgeable professionals, most of them there by invitation, and the authenticity of their goods is usually guaranteed. Expect some room for negotiation on prices on the final day of a show or market, especially if the coveted item is large in size, because many dealers would prefer to go home with an empty van.

AUCTIONS. In this unique setting, the buyer, not the seller, establishes the price of things, but it takes knowledge and discipline to come out of an auction house a winner. Many dealers are in the audience bidding on objects for themselves or for their clients, so it's important that you know what you like and what you can afford to offer for it, then stick to those limits. Even if there is a printed auction catalog, do your homework by attending the auction preview and looking carefully at the objects that interest you. Country auctions under tents are less formal than the extravaganzas orchestrated by Sotheby's and Christie's in the big city, and sometimes there are long waits before the exceptional piece is put on the block. Also, don't judge an auctioneer by his overalls—when it comes to trading in antiques, dealers in rural locations have become just as canny as their urban counterparts.

FLEA MARKETS. The average flea market consists of a wide range of purveyors of secondhand household goods, discount merchandise, collectibles, and junk of every description, spread out in tiny booths over a couple of acres, outdoors or under the roof of an abandoned shopping mall. More specialized flea markets take place in conjunction with auctions devoted to specific categories of goods. Then there are the gargantuan seasonal flea markets that require diligence and stamina to cover successfully. The Brimfield, Massachusetts, outdoor antiques show, held every May, July, and September, hosts more than 4,500 dealers. "My husband and I get in line between 5 and 5:30 A.M. to get in, then walk for six hours," observes Ohio dealer Judy Conrad. "In the spring it can be cold, raining, or snowing. It's exhausting, but it's exciting." The only way to tackle something this big is with a list of priorities, speed afoot, and readiness to make an offer. And if you make a mistake, you can always give it as a gift!

Guided by Intuition

AS A YOUNG GIRL growing up in the Arizona desert, Sharon Mrozinski filled her scrapbooks with cut-out images of New England life, an irony not lost on the dealer who today purveys Americana from an 18th-century sea captain's house in Wiscasset, Maine.

"I did not make my first trip to New England until I was an adult," Sharon admits, "but it was all that I had imagined." So much so that she can't remember a time when she was not buying, selling, or collecting New England antiques.

"I was introduced to New England on the best of terms," she says, through a visit to a friend's family home on Georgetown Island, Maine. This was an early-18th-century farmhouse, basically unchanged in spirit and in fact. "There was no running water, not telephone, and no electricity when I stayed there," Sharon recalls. "I remember the fires in the hearth, the evening presence of oil lamps, and the trips we made to the

On a circa 1820 Maine blanket chest with original gray paint, a family of vintage teddy bears keeps company with a plucky papier-mâché canine wrapped in painted cloth. OPPOSITE: A collection of painted cloth and leather balls from the mid-1800s, used for playing games like tenpins, adds graphic interest to an old Amish shelf.

well to fetch water for bathing and cooking."

The matriarch of the family had furnished the house in true Down East fashion, scrounging antiques for next to nothing, and the result was a home with authentic Yankee character. Sharon was so taken by the experience that she was almost reluctant to return home to California. When she did, she went with a plan: to open an antiques business that would satisfy her craving for New England, and finance annual buying trips to Maine.

As time went on, Sharon developed an unerring instinct for American antiques with original surfaces. "The old Yankee

mentality to keep and use everything is what has allowed these furnishings to survive to this day," she observes. Her shop in Carmel Valley was one of the few with Early American folk art and furnishings.

In 1986, she and husband Paul, an architect, moved her rapidly growing collection of painted furniture, textiles, and accessories to Wiscasset's Marston House, a Federal-style residence built in about 1785, spacious enough to serve both as home and shop. Sharon discovered in Wiscasset, Maine, a cohesive community of dealers, "a sort of collective in a village," she explains, "with each of us eager for people to visit all of us."

The shop within Marston House is

RIGHT: In a period house scant on storage, an antique leather trunk holds the owner's surplus of pillows. BELOW: The shop in Marston House, Wiscasset, Maine, exudes the atmosphere of an old general store, thanks to early mannequins, bins of fabric bolts, straw hats, and hand-painted signs. The vests are made locally by a seamstress who uses bits and pieces salvaged by the owner from old quilts. OPPOSITE: An 18th-century ship builder's level makes a graphic statement on the living room wall of antiques and textiles dealer Sharon Mrozinski. The old signs are prized for their hand-lettering and striking artwork.

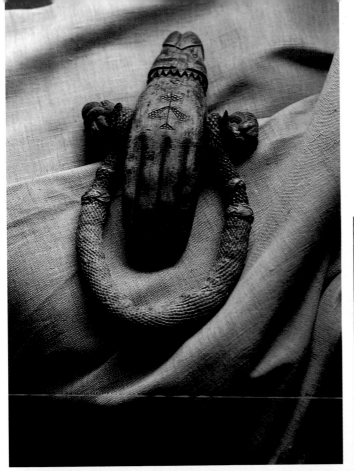

OPPOSITE: Beneath a New England hooked rug dating from the late 1800s, a set of 1820 country Windsor chairs, with original paint and decoration, stands ready for inspection.

ABOVE LEFT: One of a pair of becketts—the handle or pull found on the side of a captain's sea chest—shows the high art practiced by 18th-century sailors on ordinary items. ABOVE: An early cast-iron urn is filled with balls originally used to extract moisture from pulp in the 18th-century process of papermaking. The papier-mâché barnyard animals are contemporary. LEFT: A circa 1820 raised-panel cupboard with original paint doubles as a pantry in the keeping room, an 1850s addition to the house. A generous pine work table from England that can seat twelve is paired with centennial Windsor chairs.

ABOVE: Framed hand-colored studies of eggs from an early ornithology publication are joined by assorted old stone and alabaster balls, nesting in seedling pots on a mantel, to emphasize their common form. LEFT: A bedroom shows its New England loyalties with its barn-red walls and the old textile patterns found on the hand-painted floor and homespun-covered bed.

invitingly laid out, a neat assemblage of early painted furniture and painted smalls, quilts, homespun, ticking, hooked rugs, decoys, baskets, architectural and garden implements, weathervanes, and birdhouses. "I have never liked clutter," says Sharon, "so I've always furnished both the shop and my house sparingly. The older I get, the more I like grays and whites—fortunately, as the hair is turning quickly!"

As a dealer, Sharon lets her intuition be her guide. "You can't always believe what somebody else tells you about a piece," she observes. "Once a picker brought me a table he was sure I would love, but I didn't like a thing about it. Then I asked to look into his truck, and there I found an amazing treasure. It was the backboard of an old fan window with the glass missing, on which time and the elements had traced a kind of trompe l'oeil of a fan window. A surprise discovery like that really makes this business fun."

Sharon was always very close to her father. "I was Daddy's little girl," she notes. But when he came east to visit Sharon and Paul and their two boys for the first time, he was a bit taken aback by the timeworn furnishings in their home. "You used to have such good taste," he remarked wistfully, trying hard not to sound negative. "To Dad, all the old furniture I had collected represented poverty," Sharon laughs. "To me, it stood for things people went out to the barn to build—tables and cupboards meant for everyday use, now mellow with age but still utilitarian. That's why, even today, I'll buy a piece of old fabric just for the beautiful mend in it."

LEFT: The birds-on-a-wire sculpture was a gift to Sharon Mrozinski from her "picker." ABOVE: A chest of many drawers, originally a fixture in an Amish general store, serves a similar purpose in Marston House. The old laundry hamper with original paint and stack of early linen sheets occupies a place of honor on an antique sawbuck table, 1800–20.

The Simple Honesty of the Ordinary

TREATING ORDINARY things with respect is the focus as much of Mark McCormick's works of art as of his antiques business. His oil paintings celebrate the sights "other people would trip over before they noticed," such as the old picket fences that wobble cheerfully through the rural countryside surrounding his home near the tiny hamlet of St. Jacob, Illinois. Dealing in antiques, Mark prefers furniture that shows it has not been influenced by worldly style or fashion. He is enamored of cupboards, dry sinks, hutches, tables, and folk art pieces made on the farm for local use long ago and far away from the cities and towns where carpenters and cabinet-makers toiled in more formal traditions. "It's the unadorned honesty of the objects that we like," he says.

The tradition of country living comes naturally both to Mark and his wife, Lisa. "We grew up here and our families still live in the area," Mark says. The couple finds inspiration in vistas others might regard as

Turn-of-the-century crockery bowls take on the quality of a still life when set out on an 1850 Illinois stepback cupboard, its history vividly recorded in layers of old paint. OPPOSITE: In a house celebrating the heritage of rural life, untouched painted country furniture and folk art creations include an 1840 dry sink and miniature house, both decorated with diamond details, a symbol of good luck for their German-born builders, and a 1920s tribute to the pastime of bridge fishing.

mundane or even desolate. "When I look out at all these fields of corn," he says, "I get the same feeling of awe as I do sitting on the beach, staring out at the sea."

Their farmhouse, built in 1858, was originally part of an 80-acre tract first tilled by a family of early German settlers. The white-painted brick facade of the house has a two-door front entry. "Originally," says Mark, "one door led into the parlor, which was for 'company only,' and the other door led to the living room, for 'children only.' They had big families back then," he adds.

On the property is a sycamore as old as the house, "so big it takes three people to reach around its trunk, with limbs stretching over the house that are themselves as thick as tree trunks," Mark notes. Lisa's spacious garden is a riot of color in the summer, with old-fashioned flowers like coxcomb, globe amaranth, sunflowers, and giant hollyocks that reach thirteen feet high. Even Lucy, their six-year-old daughter, has a stake in the garden. "She's created a modest seed business, called 'Lucy's Seeds,' and anything she earns goes into Lucy's pony fund," says Mark.

The McCormick decorating style is simple: they like things that look good in their house, and that make their house look good in turn. To further this synchronicity, the couple decided to enliven the house by painting rooms in soft colors, easy to live with. "They're colors that don't close in on you," Mark explains, and they make an ideal background for their furniture.

The versatility of farm-made furnishings is demonstrated by an 1850 dry sink used as a buffet, a jelly cupboard made into a storage closet, and a rustic table commandeered as a baking center. The boldly articulated images of a favorite daily ritual are the work of owner Mark McCormick.

BELOW: The curving head and foot of an Arts and Crafts–style bed and a miniature cottage with a genuine stone facade, made by a local folk architect, give a sense of grace and repose to the master bedroom. RIGHT: Brought inside, a patio furniture set enjoys its upgrade amid folk art and painted primitive furnishings.

In the house, the couple feels free to mix styles and periods, blending a suite of 1930s outdoor furniture, for example, with pieces from the 1830s, along with works of contemporary art. "It all works for us because we like things with good color and form," Mark says, and it is convenient, suiting the revolving-door ownership that is the trademark of the antiques dealer life. "You can't get too sentimental about things," says Mark, "because we're always moving them along."

That's not to say there aren't some things he and Lisa would like to hold on to, such as an 1840 dry sink that seems to belong with their house. It was originally painted red, then repainted blue and mustard, and has a diamond motif, a German symbol of good luck. And Lucy won't part with her collection—more than one hundred pint-size pastel-colored McCoy flowerpots.

The McCormicks have had their share of good luck in the business, especially for being so young at the game. Now in their thirties, they have been selling antiques for more than a decade. "We found that we really got a charge out of finding something really good and then selling it to someone who appreciated it just as much," says Mark. They travel to between ten and seventeen shows a year, and it's often a family affair. At a recent show, Mark presided over a selection of painted American antiques in one booth. Next door, in a booth delineated by a small picket fence, mother and daughter were busy selling Lisa's fresh flower bouquets, Lucy's seeds, and an array of tiny treasures.

ABOVE: A corner of the house draws attention with hand-hewn treasures such as the bent willow chair, a Northwest Indian totem pole from the 1920s, and a flock of birds old and new, including the five-foot-tall portrait of a chicken, a creation of the owner. LEFT: The painted collage on woven paper was an anniversary Valentine from Mark to Lisa.

Jacqueline and Douglas Eichhorn have filled their 19th-century home with the quirky relics of eras past and present, including a metal platter-spinning weathervane by Joe Burden. OPPOSITE: Shelves lined with 1950s–60s "prison art" boxes and frames (made from folded cigarette packages), a neighbor's folk art animal figures, and a polychromed carved head reflect the couple's eclectic tastes.

JESU
MAY-CO
TODA

The Richness of the Unusual in Daily Life

FOR JACQUELINE AND DOUGLAS Eichhorn, the passion for folk art that now permeates their lives in Centerville, Indiana, was first sparked when they worked as Peace Corps volunteers in Peru in the 1960s. Here, they discovered the riches of the Incan culture and the legacy of native crafts. "I knew I could never afford to buy a Miró," Jackie observes, "but I could own a piece of admirable folk art."

The Eichhorns moved to Centerville in 1969 when Douglas joined the faculty at nearby Earlham College to teach literature and creative writing. The community of 3,500 had been a thriving county seat in the 1800s, but lost much of its importance and luster when the railroad bypassed it in favor of another town, Richmond.

"The buildings are what attracted us," Jackie says. "Most of them were built between 1800 and 1840, when Centerville really was a center—a beehive of activity for lawyers and land speculators. The 'National Road,' one of America's first high-

ways, was used by wagon trains heading west. It passes through the center of town, and becomes 'Main Street' inside the town limits."

When Centerville ceased to serve as the county seat, its economy fell into a long decline. Oddly enough, the hard times may have helped to preserve the original buildings. "People didn't have the money to tear down houses and build new ones," Jackie explains, "so for such a small town, we have a remarkably high number of vintage 19th-century brick and frame buildings still standing."

The Eichhorns live in one of them, a two-story Federal-style brick building, originally Gentry's Saddlery and Wagon Shop. Surrounded by reminders of the original frontier, the couple push a new frontier in collecting the household products of the postwar 1940s and 1950s—the objects they believe will become tomorrow's desirable antiques and collectibles.

"The people who bought these items when they were new, whether furniture, toys, tools, or other things, are now at the end of their lives," Jackie observes. "As their households are broken up, their possessions are coming into the marketplace." The Eichhorns are not interested in every enamel kitchen table that shows up. They look for things that are unusual in themselves, such as a one-of-a-kind papier-mâché folk figure, or things that specifically evoke the period, such as a Charles Eames plywood chair, or a molded fiberglass chair, or a Harry Bertovan wire chair, or things that have accrued value and interest because they've become outmoded, such as LP record albums (made obsolete by compact disks, but important historical and artistic documents for their covers as well as for the recorded music).

ABOVE: The scale model, measuring four square feet, of a prominent manufacturer's home—the Garr Mansion in Richmond, Indiana—makes an impressive architectural miniature inside the Eichhorn house. RIGHT: Bought locally, the "courting" gift is a work of tramp art created out of cedar cigar boxes with polychromed heart decoration. OPPOSITE: Midcentury Americana that promises to become tomorrow's valued antiques includes face jugs by fifth-generation northern Georgia potter Grace Nell Hewell, sheet music from movie musicals, wooden trucks carved by a trucker while he was laid off during the 1980s recession, and molded plywood Charles Eames coffee table and chairs from the 1940s.

Figures that are featured prominently in the Eichhorns' collection include "Sidney," ABOVE, a homemade ventriloquist's dummy that came complete with Prohibition Era scripts, and "Mattie," BELOW, a statuesque carved and polychromed matron. RIGHT: Airplanes made from Coke and Pepsi containers dominate the airspace in one upstairs room of the Eichhorn house, while a Moxie girl looks on. OPPOSITE: Collected today for their color and shape, plastic "Boonton" dishes were the dinnerware of choice in many American households in the 1940s and 1950s. The working kitchen is true to its retro school, right down to the 1960s electric range.

"We've bought almost everything in our house within a radius of one hundred miles of Centerville," Jackie Eichhorn explains, "so our things largely reflect the local culture, edited by our quirky preferences. We're not collectors in the sense of predetermining what we want and then going out and searching for it. We acquire things as we happen on them, or they on us."

With their eye for the unorthodox, the Eichhorns have begun collecting the work of a fourteen-year-old boy from a nearby farm, who makes human and animal figures out of discarded farm implements, using old sparkplugs for eyes. "It's not so different from the process the old quilt makers used," Jackie points out, "piecing together their works or art from whatever scraps of cloth happened to be at hand." She adds that, while quilts may hold appeal for people of one generation, a younger generation may not see them in the same light. For many younger collectors, artifacts from more recent times beckon.

Indiana's fertile soil has made it a major agricultural state. Jackie relates that the few natural areas that have escaped the plow are those "small remnants and fragments too steep, too wet, or too dry to 'turn to account,' as the farmers say. These are the places I love the most, but it takes a determined special interest to find them."

As collectors, the Eichhorns turn to account the flotsam and jetsam of daily life that others overlook.

the next Wave

"Antique" and "collectible" are relative terms. "When I first started out as a dealer in the 1960s," says Jack Adamson, "the 1880s were considered 'late.' Now, that decade is considered 'early.' When we turn into the 21st century, a lot of things will suddenly seem old."

Jackie and Doug Eichhorn are dealers who grew up in the Midwest in the 1960s. Jackie observes that for their parents, Early American maple was the wood furniture of choice. "Architects and designers were the only ones dealing with new design," she explains, such as the Eames plywood chair and George Nelson furniture. Looking ahead, Jackie believes that the generation now moving into collecting will probably reject "all those interiors crammed with baskets and quilts," because those things are not part of their collective memory.

Here are the collectibles of the future, the objects that can be found at flea markets and junk shops that will increase in value and appreciation in the years to come, according to many of the collectors and dealers featured in this book. (Not surprisingly, our sources all hasten to add, "Buyer, beware—there is no guarantee all predictions will pan out.")

ALBUM COVERS FROM THE 1960S (ROCK 'N' ROLL). "The CD format that made album covers obsolete has now made them collectible," notes Eichhorn.

ARTIFACTS FROM THE 1970S, as "boomer" pop culture is coming on strong—don't throw away your beanbag chairs.

ARTIFACTS OF THE COWBOY WEST, from old spurs and saddles to diner dishware sporting ranch brands to Roy Rogers lunch boxes.

BAKELITE PRODUCTS such as radios, flatware, and jewelry made in the 1920s and '30s to simulate ivory, tortoiseshell, or wood surfaces.

COTTAGE SHUTTERS WITH CUTOUT MOTIFS such as stars, pinecones, quarter moons, acorns, and sailboats.

ENAMELWARE FOR COOKING, SERVING, AND STORING—staples of the American kitchen from the 1870s to the 1930s and made and marketed under various names, including spackleware, porcelainware, and graniteware.

FURNITURE WITH ORIGINAL PAINT—peeling and weathered, the mellower the better, on chairs, cupboards, and tables.

HOTEL SILVER TABLEWARE, made for durability and with simple lines, for luxury hotels, ocean liners, first-class trains, cafés, and restaurants.

LOVING CUP TROPHIES from school competitions, country club tournaments, regattas, and other sporting events.

"MIDCENTURY MODERN" glassware, pottery (especially from the Arts and Crafts movement, such as the work of Russel Wright, and lesser-known Red Wing from Minnesota), textiles, and furnishings (everything from Lava Lamps to Charles Eames chairs and Heywood-Wakefield birch and maple furniture), from the 1930s to the early 1960s.

QUILTS FROM THE 1880S TO THE 1930S (earlier quilts are rare and very expensive).

SCHOOLGIRL ART such as painted boxes, theorem paintings, cut-paper assemblages, and other crafts and artwork executed by young women in the late 19th and early 20th centuries.

SMOKING PARAPHERNALIA, including advertising signs, lighters, ashtrays, and cigarette stands.

SPORTING FOLK ART such as Indian clubs, barbells, and walking sticks, vintage baseball equipment (especially balls, catcher's masks, mitts, and children's gloves), and figurative shooting gallery targets.

TRAVEL SOUVENIRS from the heyday of ocean liner and rail travel: posters, destination postcards, vintage luggage (especially when it is covered with labels of exotic locales or posh hotels and spas), World's Fair memorabilia, plates commemorating states, and miscellaneous tokens of vacation travel such as Native American beaded pincushions, snowdomes, and miniature landmarks.

WIRE HOUSEHOLD PRODUCTS such as potato mashers, bottle carriers, and dish drainers; also commercial wire utensils such as clam baskets.

WORLD GLOBES—records of our ever-changing international lineup.

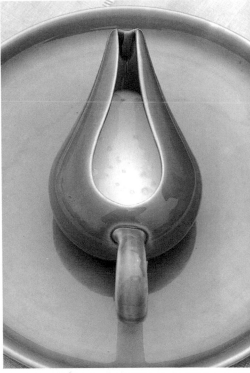

Keeping the Faith

A FINE LINE SEPARATES dealer from collector. Both buy with the same passion, perhaps. But while the collector can't imagine parting with the object of desire, the dealer can't afford to keep it. Gloria List who plunged into dealing in antiques over two decades ago with a $5,000 investment in quilts, spells it out clearly: "It's how I make my living."

Gloria recalls the advice she received once when she was working for an art dealer on Madison Avenue in New York. Invited to his home for dinner, Gloria was puzzled to discover the dealer had no paintings on his walls. She asked him, "How can it be? You deal in such wonderful art, yet there's none of it here?"

"Unless you have a trust fund or a wealthy patron," he told her, "there's no way to make a living as an art dealer if you start buying art for yourself." The same, Gloria feels, applies to dealing in antiques.

A 1970s quilt exhibit at the Whitney Museum of American Art is what

A carved saint from Guatemala, with moveable arms and drop earrings, is the centerpiece of a room in antiques dealer Gloria List's adobe home in Santa Fe. The lifesize Christ from Mexico and the hands with a silver Sacred Heart in their grasp both date from the 19th century.

OPPOSITE: A late-19th-century Mexican *trastero* is crowned with a pair of ecclesiastical tin flower vessels, a 19th-century Mexican *cristo* with rosary beads, and a piece of New Mexican crafts pottery from the 1930s.

inspired Gloria to go into business for herself. "The graphic images these 19th-century women had sewn and composed in their quilts were so powerful to me," she recalls, and she knew others would have the same reaction if she could find a way to underline the fact that quilts deserved to be collected as art. She began buying old quilts. When she had assembled about five hundred specimens, she rented a small store-front for $450 a month (in a location that would cost ten times that amount today), hung quilts on all the walls, and opened Nonesuch Gallery.

"That's when cold fear seized me," she recalls. "I suddenly thought to myself, What if no one else sees my quilts as works of art?"

Gloria had no reason to worry, as collectors and designers flocked to her shop and purchased the quilts. Her business was off and running.

When she moved to California, she started operating her business out of her home. "I said to myself, 'You can't open a quilt shop in Los Angeles—who walks?'" A later move, to Santa Monica, put None-such Gallery back on the street, this time reflecting the culture of the region Gloria had moved to and thoroughly absorbed. Quilts now took a backseat to an eclectic

inventory of American Indian artifacts, Navajo weavings, cowboy paraphernalia, and Mexican folk art from the 19th century to the 1930s. Gloria also dealt in paintings commissioned by the

Works Progress Administration during the Depression.

Today, the religious art and artifacts from Mexico, New Mexico, Central America, and Spain are the focus of Gloria's business. Having moved to Santa Fe in 1993, she now deals exclusively from her home, where it's easy for her to show clients how materials originally meant for use in a house of worship can have such a strong impact in a house of one's own. "Most people have never seen religious art used out of context," she notes. "But when you combine a statue of a saint with a retablo, some Mexican artifacts and weavings, and a Navajo blanket, it becomes a

ABOVE: Mimicking the custom of home altars, the dealer assembled a grouping of religious works. The painting of Mary in the gold-leaf frame is a product of the 18th-century Peruvian Cuzco School. It is surrounded by a processional lantern from Italy, a large articulated figure of St. Joseph, and a painted and gessoed figure of St. José. LEFT: An old ladder from a pueblo and an iron New Mexico cross cast their shadows in an otherwise bare courtyard. RIGHT: A turn-of-century Christ figure dominates a room furnished with 18th-century Mexican religious art and artifacts, including a painting of Madonna and Child and a hand of Christ with stigmata.

TOP: A pair of carved 18th-century wood angels float gracefully on Cloud Nine in a kitchen as well stocked with religious art as with food. The turn-of-the-century New Mexican *trastero* is decked with *milagros* and Sacred Hearts. The imposing terracotta finial was retrieved from a 19th-century building in Kansas City.

ABOVE: Lending their striking forms to a sleek bathroom are a Mexican gold leaf carving and a 19th-century American column topped with a carved stone piece and an urn with ball.

kind of secular art of its own, still with spiritual underpinnings."

Gloria enjoys helping her clients gain a deeper appreciation for their specialized interests. She is one dealer who does not hesitate to share what she knows. "I've learned a lot from the collectors I've met," she says, "and I'm always happy to pass along that information to others. I'll send my clients to other dealers whom I respect, if it will help them find what they are looking for, because I know that all of us will benefit in the end."

Not every interior can accommodate a life-size crucifix. Altar candlesticks, chalices, and monstrances are more manageable in size, as are religious paintings of Mexican Colonial vintage, with their gold-leaf pigments and rich landscape backgrounds.

The area where Gloria lives reinforces the enthusiasm she feels for her present collecting focus. "I live in an Hispanic neighborhood and am always hearing the Spanish language," she says. "My neighbor and I like to drive out into the villages to visit the tiny churches where the faith is still practiced."

Faith also shines through in the art that Gloria responds to most fervently. "A naive, almost crude, portrait of a religious figure can be beautiful," she observes, "because it reflects the love and adoration that the artist felt when he applied his tiny pieces of tin to the image."

Clients are always asking Gloria, "How can you sell this beautiful saint?"

"I tell them that I'm lucky to be making a living from selling beautiful art and sculpture," she relates, "and if passing something along gives someone else great pleasure, so much the better."

At least, she has the beauty for a time. *Sic transit gloria.*

In a living room overflowing with fascinating religious folk art and rustic furniture, one unusual object stands out: an image of Our Lady of Guadalupe fashioned from dried flowers and once carried in Easter processionals.

religious art of New Mexico

For the early Spanish settlers of the New Mexico Territory, religion was the strongest link to the homeland. A vital crafts movement grew out of the building and furnishing of churches and homes, as villagers carved figures of saints from cottonwood; painted religious portraits, using tempera colors made from indigenous clay and minerals; and wove altar cloths with homespun wool dyed with indigo, brazilwood, and other native plants.

"There is no academic background for santero art," says Santa Fe dealer Gloria List. "It is very honest, expressing devotion in a simple, innocent, yet moving and dignified way, and the colors are beautiful."

Tin became a common medium for the village artists with the opening of the Santa Fe Trail in the 1840s. They recycled empty tins originally used for lamp oil, lard, and other supplies, pounding, punching, and painting the material into religious ornamental pieces. These tin crafts indicate the last period of New Mexican arts.

Here is an abbreviated guide to the most common terms of New Mexico santero village art.

ANGELITO. Paintings or carvings of angel figures, often no more than a round face and stubby butterfly wings.

BULTO. A painted statue of a saint, carved out of cottonwood, constructed of separate components held together with pegs and glue, and sometimes embellished with plaster of paris to add more detailed expression, human hair, and deeply carved skirts and robes. Smaller bultos could be removed from the church for religious celebrations or to carry into the homes of the sick and dying for comfort.

CRISTO. The "Man of Sorrows," a life-size carved figure of the crucified Christ, with a face infused with great sadness, hands and feet sensitively represented, and wounds and streams of blood presented with Medieval directness. This icon was the crowning achievement of a village artist.

EX VOTO. A small votive picture, or "story painting," executed on canvas or tin to commemorate a healing experience or other miracle; along with a brief description of the event, it was placed in church as a public offer of thanks.

NICHO. A carved wood or punched tin shelf or cabinet ranging in style from plain to ornate, that held or displayed religious objects. When used in the home, *nichos* contained household saints who protected the family from misfortune.

REREDOS. An altar-back framework for exhibiting paintings or niches for sculpture.

RETABLO. A small religious painting by a native artist, usually painted on a board of seasoned pine or cottonwood coated with gesso (gypsum plaster), with natural clay pigments; after 1850 they were also made on tin and with oil paints.

SANTERO. Native religious artist of New Mexico. The earliest *santeros* were Franciscan missionaries, who taught villagers how to paint and carve; many *santeros* traveled from village to village in the New Mexico Territory, selling their homemade *santos*. These artists in turn passed their skills on to their sons.

SANTO. General term for any depiction, whether painting, sculpture, or print, of the divine persons, saints, or events of the Catholic Church. The small *santos* that once guarded their New Mexican adobes from carved wooden niches in the house were a central part of daily life. The family might curry favor with gifts of candles or other offerings. If the *santo* failed to deliver on the wish or prayer, however, the family might well punish the *santo* by turning it to face the wall or locking it in a chest for a period of time.

Guessing the Next Trend

TO SUCCEED AS AN antiques dealer, you need a crystal ball (preferably, of course, an antique one).

That's the view of Rod Lich and Susan Parrett, who have been buying and selling antiques together for as long as they've been married, some two decades. They conduct business out of a 19th-century farmhouse, on the Indiana side of the Ohio River, a mere fifteen-minute drive from downtown Louisville, Kentucky.

"We're constantly looking ahead to the future, asking ourselves, 'What's the next trend in the market?'" says Rod. Antique shows provide them with the best barometer on trends and price points. "At a show, a thousand qualified customers are going to respond to what we have on the floor in a single day," he explains. "In a shop, it may take weeks and even months to get that kind of feedback. You find out right away what is hot."

Their business has evolved over the years, although there are certain

The basketmaking craft of three generations of the McAdams family earns a place of honor atop a walnut cupboard. The painting on tin is an early advertisement for the railroad line that once ran between Chicago and Nashville. OPPOSITE: Snappy turtle stepstools add dash and wit to an 1840s farmhouse.

TOP: **The living room is enlivened with a late-19th-century Victorian silk crib quilt, made in Indiana, and a South Carolina table with its original paint still intact.** ABOVE: **Originally white and beige, the stairs were given a creative finger-painted treatment by the owners to hide the scars of traffic from the household's four dogs.** INSET: **The stars-and-heart-decorated tramp art frame was fashioned by an Indianapolis carver out of walnut at the turn of the century.**

constants. "When we started out, we specialized in quilts and country furniture," says Susan. "Today, we're heavily into hickory furniture. The market is always in flux."

Early-20th-century or Depression-era quilts lost some of their value when imported reproductions crowded the market. Now, as collectors realize that the new products do not hold up, the vintage quilts are again appreciated for their richness of color and pattern and their ability to stand the test of time.

Hickory furniture was long a staple of manufacturing in Indiana, where hickory trees flourished. It was made from 1899 to 1940, with the heyday of the form coming during the 1920s. Collectors respond to its sturdiness, natural color, and rustic look.

Its original appeal was that it did not look as if it belonged in a Victorian parlor. "The factories shipped the furniture all over the country," says Rod, "wherever there were camps,  lodges, second homes." The great camps of the Adirondacks and the Western lodges of the national parks were all furnished with Indiana hickory.

"Collectors buy with the heart, dealers buy with the mind," Rod observes, and this contrast is reflected in the couple.

Susan has loved antiques since she was a child. While at Earlham College, she and a roommate sold quilts. They saved their profits in a glass jar, our "antiques store fund," she recalls. Her long-standing love of old things is why some items she has collected, such as the folk art parrots (of special appeal to her because of her name), aren't for sale. She also treasures

The old map and topographical print for a New Albany steamship company are both dated 1831; on the table is a grouping of Indiana limestone whimsies, the work of monument carvers.

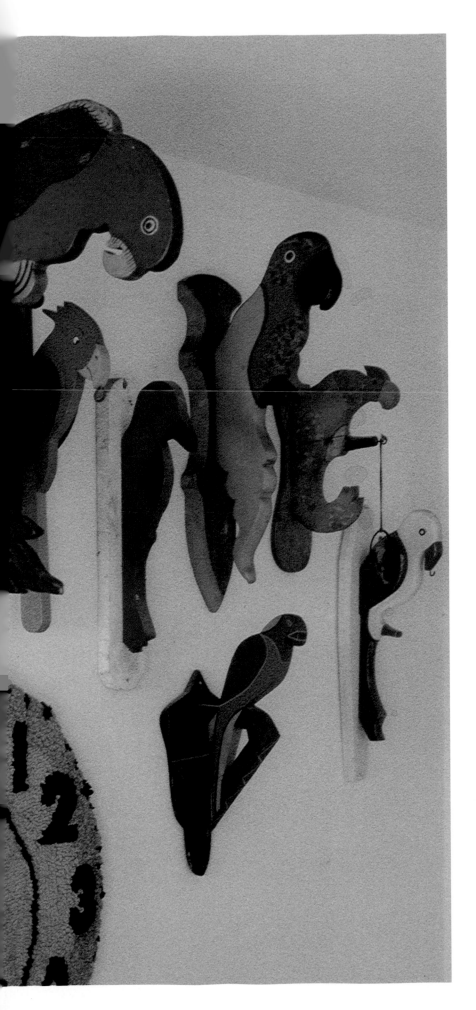

anything with original surface color, such as the yellow ladderback chairs from a Kentucky cabin, the venerable green kitchen cupboard from southern Indiana, the red-dog standing ashtray from the 1930s, and the blue-green hunt board from North Carolina.

Some of Susan's collections have come by chance. At one of the first auctions she attended, she bid on four small, deep-woven baskets with handles. They appealed to her because, although they were utility baskets, they had the elegance of ladies' handbags. "After I bought them, I found out they were related!" Susan says—made by three generations of the McAdams family in Harrison County. Today, Susan has more than thirty examples of McAdams craftsmanship.

Rod brought his schooling in retail management to the business when they married. "I appreciate what Susan responds to in objects, and I also like having things around me that I enjoy," he explains. "But I'll look at an item on the investment level, figuring out its sales potential." He won't acquire a piece unless its physical condition is as good as its other merits. Recently, he was tempted by a rare bottle whimsy, but the figures of coal miners inside the vessel had fallen down and there was no way to repair them. "It just wasn't there for me anymore."

When something is "there," however, both Rod and Susan feel the elation of discovery. Not long ago a retired dealer sent them snapshots of some unusual figures he had seen offered at a farm sale in Iowa. The couple found the figures intriguing enough to drive nine hours to

The original talking heads, parrot pot hooks made in high school shop classes in the 1940s and 1950s, came to Susan Parrett mostly as gifts from friends acknowledging her evocative surname.

see them. Made entirely out of bottlecaps, they were fashioned to resemble animals, space aliens, and other creatures, and all stood between three and four feet high. A tenant farmer had made them for his own amusement, stowing them in his barn.

Forty-five bottlecap figures went from the Iowa barn to Rod and Susan's barn. Susan responded to them as comical folk art. Rod saw them as "fresh merchandise that hadn't been shopped around." Both were right. Within months they had sold them all. Today, the tenant farmer's handiwork is found in galleries, commanding $4,000 to $7,000 a figure.

ABOVE: A token of affection by a tramp art craftsman. LEFT: In the kitchen, traditional Hoosier hospitality is expressed in commodious cupboards that bring charm and storage capacity to their surroundings. The raised diamond design on the three-door cupboard indicates the Germanic heritage of its southern Indiana builder. BELOW: Only five minutes from downtown Louisville, the Parrett-Lich homestead evinces traditional Ohio River Valley farm life. OPPOSITE: A glass-fronted painted walnut cupboard from southern Indiana, dated 1850, overflows with jugtown pottery from Seagrove, North Carolina.

LEFT: Made by Preacher Ben Davis, this one-of-a-kind bed was built of twigs harvested from North Carolina rhododendron, mountain laurel, and willow. Folk art on a smaller scale includes a collection of nuthead and cloth dolls arranged on a shelf supported by old brackets. RIGHT: A bathroom with a window on the outdoors is furnished with rustic antiques like the Indian ladderback chair, used to keep extra towels at hand. BELOW LEFT: Hoosier antiques rule the upstairs master bedroom roost in the form of a Wabash chest of drawers, a Petersburg chair, and a southern Indiana hired man's quilt. BELOW RIGHT: A bottle whimsy from 1904 celebrates a home craft of the day.

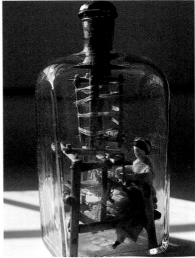

Resource guide

ALABAMA

Bodiford's Antique Mall
919 Hampton Street
Montgomery, AL 36106
334-265-4220
Furniture, glassware, crystal,
porcelain

Robert Cargo Folk Art Gallery
2314 6th Street
Tuscaloosa, AL 35401
205-758-8884
Folk art, paintings, sculptures, 20th-
century African-American quilts. By
appointment only.

ARIZONA

Razzberries
7033 E. Indian School Road
Scottsdale, AZ 85251
602-990-9047
Antiques, pre-owned furniture, tas-
sels, trims, lamps, treasures

ARKANSAS

Hogan's Antique Furniture
14502 Cantrell Road
Little Rock, AR 72212
501-868-9224
Eclectic furnishings, glassware

Potential Treasures Antiques
700 N. Van Buren Street
Little Rock, AR 72205
501-663-0608

Traditional 19th- and 20th-century
antiques, vintage linen, lamps, mir-
rors, sterling, crystal, china

CALIFORNIA

Aero
207 Ocean Avenue
Laguna Beach, CA 92651
714-376-0535
19th-century Mission Revival archi-
tectural pieces, American arts and
crafts

American Roots
105 W. Chapman
Orange, CA 92666
714-639-3424
American country antiques, toys,
quilts, garden accessories, folk art,
architectural elements

East Meets West Antiques
658 North Larchmont Blvd.
Hollywood, CA 90004
213-461-1389
Antiques, accessories, quilts, textiles,
country furnishings, Americana

Hunt Antiques
478 Jackson Street
San Francisco, CA 94111
415-989-9531
Antique furniture, fine art, acces-
sories. By appointment only.

Wild Goose Chase &
    Sweet William
1936 South Coast Highway

Laguna Beach, CA 92651
714-376-9388
Antique Americana, quilts, beacon
blankets, pre-1900 antiques, painted
furniture

Brenda Cain
1211 Montana Avenue
Santa Monica, CA 90403
310-395-1559
Antiques, jewelry, 20th-century
textiles, pottery, furniture

COLORADO

38 Antiques Ltd.
520 East Hyman Avenue
Aspen, CO 81611
303-925-5885
Antiques, 17th- to 19th-century fur-
niture, garden statues, Venetian and
Florentine pieces, reproductions from
England and France

CONNECTICUT

EGH Peter, Inc.
Box 52
Norfolk, CT 06058
203-542-5221
American 18th- and 19th-century painted furniture and folk art, emphasis on original finishes

DELAWARE

Bellefont Resale Shop
4000 N. Market Street
Wilmington, DE 19802
302-762-1885
Antique clocks, hall tables, Mission oak furniture, oil lamps

F.H. Herman Antiques
308 Philadelphia Pike
Wilmington, DE 19809
302-764-5333
Porcelain, furniture, silver, art glass. By appointment only.

Twice Nice Antiques
5714 Kennett Pike
Centreville, DE 19807
302-656-8881
Chippendale, Federal, Queen Anne furnishings and accessories

Wamboz
174 Rehoboth Avenue
Rehoboth, DE 19977
800-669-9426
Sofas, chairs, lamps, clocks, tables, pottery, flatware

FLORIDA

Antiques & Things
515 Fleming Street
Key West, FL 33040
305-292-1333
Furniture, glassware, stuffed animals, jewelry, furniture, prints, and paintings

Wisteria Corner Antique Mall
225 North Main
High Springs, FL 32643
904-454-3555
American and European antiques, collectibles, hand-crafted items

GEORGIA

Atlanta Antiques Exchange
1185 Howell Mill Road NW
Atlanta, GA 30318
404-351-0727
19th- and 20th-century English, Oriental, Continental pottery and porcelain

Jacqueline Adams Antiques
2300 Peachtree Road NW
Atlanta, GA 30309
404-355-8123
Country and French antiques, porcelain, crystal/silver, antique garden accessories

Levison & Cullen Gallery
(Deanne Levison)
2300 Peachtree Road
Suite C-101
Atlanta, GA 30309
404-351-3435
*American antique and decorative
art from 18th and 19th centuries,
collectibles*

IDAHO
Michel's Inc.
P.O. Box 1597
Sun Valley, ID 83353
208-726-8382
French and English country antiques

Sioux Antiques
8 North Main Street
P.O. Box 635
Victor, ID 83455
208-787-2644
*Rustic furniture, Western oak and
pine furniture, antique kitchen
accessories*

ILLINOIS
Harvey Antiques
123 Chicago Avenue
Evanston, IL 60202
708-866-6766
*18th- and 19th-century American
furnishings, folk art*

Joanne Boardman Antiques
522 Joanne Lane
Dekalb, IL 60115
815-756-9359
*Country furniture and accessories,
New England painted furniture*

Mark & Lisa McCormick
8837 Schmalz
St. Jacob, IL 62281
618-667-7789
*Folk art, painted antique furniture,
paintings by Mark McCormick*

Frank & Barbara Pollack
1214 Green Bay Road
Highland Park, IL 60035
708-433-2213
*American antiques and art. By
appointment only.*

INDIANA
Heirloom Antiques
3414 N. Shadeland Avenue #C
Indianapolis, IN 46226
317-542-8700
*Antique ink wells, dolls, Victorian
accessories, glassware, Royal Dalton,
German beer steins. By appointment only.*

Indianapolis Downtown
    Antiques
1044 Virginia Avenue
Indianapolis, IN 46203
317-635-5336
*1900 to 1930s furniture, Hummels,
Royal Dalton, blue/white stoneware,
McCoy pottery, oak furniture*

Recollections Antiques
5202 N. College Avenue
Indianapolis, IN 46220
317-283-3800
*Eclectic furniture, linens, musical
instruments, crockery*

Doug & Jackie Eichhorn
Webb's Antique Mall
200 Union Street
Centerville, IN 47330
317-855-2489
*20th-century American folk art, late-
1940s to 1950s American designer
furniture and accessories*

Rod Lich & Susan Parrett
2164 Canal Lane
Georgetown, IN 47122
812-738-1858
*Folk art, rustic furniture, American
country furniture. By appointment
only.*

IOWA

Snusville Antiques
852 Hull Avenue
Des Moines, IA 50316
515-265-5799
Eclectic antiques

Bartlett's Quilts
820 35th Street
Des Moines, IA 50312
515-255-1362
Quilts

KANSAS

Antique Plaza of Topeka
2935 SW Topeka Boulevard
Topeka, KS 66611
913-267-7411
*American country furniture, fine
Victorian furniture, Galle glassware,
cut glass, Rose Point glass*

Family Affair Antique Mall
3300 West Sixth Avenue SW
Topeka, KS 66604
913-233-8822
*Depression glass, 1920s to 1930s
furniture, tea sets, Matchbox
cars, toys*

Old World Antiques Ltd.
4436 State Line Road
Kansas City, KS 66103
913-677-4744
*French Old World antiques, furnish-
ings, accessories*

KENTUCKY

Den of Steven Antiques Mall
945 Baxter Avenue
Louisville, KY 40204
505-458-9581
Eclectic furnishings (Federal, Victorian, English, French), china, silver, crystal

Ruth C. Scully Antiques
5237 Bardstown Road
Louisville, KY 40291
502-491-9601
Early-19th-century furniture, decorative arts, textiles, Nantucket baskets, folk art, Staffordshire figures. By appointment only.

Yesterday Antiques
P.O. Box 135
Burgin, KY 40310
606-748-5588
Country and primitive furniture and accessories

LOUISIANA

Mac Maison, Ltd.
3963 Magazine Street
New Orleans, LA 70115
504-891-2863
Antiques, lighting, architectural artifacts, ornamentations

Wirthmore Antiques
5723 Magazine Street
New Orleans, LA 70015
504-897-9727
18th- and 19th-century French Provincial furniture

MAINE

Marston House
Main Street
Wiscasset, ME 04578
207-882-6010
Primarily late-18th- and 19th-century furniture in original paint, accessories, textiles

Riverbank Antiques
Wells Union Antique Center
   on Rt. 1
Wells, ME 07090
207-646-6314
English, French, Italian garden architectural elements and decorative antiques

Barbara Doherty
P.O. Box 974
Kennebunkport, ME 04046
207-967-4673
18th-century country furniture and folk art. By appointment only.

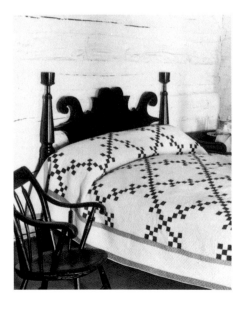

MARYLAND

All of Us Americans Folk Art
Box 30440
Bethesda, MD 20824
301-652-4626
Southern antique furniture, wood figures, quilts, paintings, weather vanes, Native American items. By appointment only.

Annapolis Antique Shop
20 Riverview Avenue
Annapolis, MD 21401
410-266-5550
Eclectic furnishings and accessories

Another Period In Time
1708 Fleet Street
Baltimore, MD 21231
410-675-4776
1780s to 1950s furniture, including Chippendale and Victorian

Antique Galleria
853 N. Howard Street
Baltimore, MD 21201
410-462-6365
Eclectic accessories, including English china, art deco, silver plate, pottery

MASSACHUSETTS

As Time Goes By
12 Parker Street
Springfield, MA 01151
413-596-4553
Collectibles, glassware, country, period pieces from the '30s and '40s. By appointment only.

Boston Antique Center, Inc.
54 Canal Street
Boston, MA 02114
614-742-1400
18th- to 20th-century quality pieces, paintings, silver, porcelain, mirrors, Oriental rugs, kilims

Commonwealth Antiques
121 Charles Street
Boston, MA 02114
617-720-1605
Textiles, sterling, lighting, old porcelain, garden accessories

Market Place Antiques
2 Wilmont Street
Springfield, MA 01108
413-732-0206
Arts and antiques, 1950s modern

MICHIGAN

Antiques Mall of Ann Arbor
2739 Plymouth Road
Ann Arbor, MI 48105
313-663-8200
Victorian, Modernist furniture, specialized pottery

Rage of the Age
314 South Ashley Street
Ann Arbor, MI 48104
313-662-0777
Vintage antique clothing and textiles

Slightly Tarnished-Used Goods
2006 E. Michigan Avenue
Lansing, MI 48912
517-485-3599
*Variety of used goods, including
antique lamps and furniture*

Judith George and Adrian Cote
14833 Birth North Shore Drive
Vandallia, MI 49095
616-476-9583
Southwestern antiques

MINNESOTA

Antiques Minnesota
1197 University Avenue West
St. Paul, MN 55104
612-646-0037
*Glassware, pottery, ceramics, furni-
ture, jewelry, toys*

Past, Present, Future
336 E. Franklin Avenue
Minneapolis, MN 55404
612-870-0702
*Vintage office furniture, Mission
oak, antique building materials. By
appointment only.*

Yankee Peddler Antiques
5008 Xerxes Avenue South
Minneapolis, MN 55410
612-926-1732
Primitive American antiques

MISSOURI

Antiques & More
2309 Cherokee Street
St. Louis, MO 63118
314-773-1150
*1850s to 1960s furniture, Limoge,
cut glass, signs, art pottery*

Cummings Corner
1703 West 45th Street
Kansas City, MO 64111
816-753-5353
*1940s Americana, restored light
fixtures, quilts*

English Garden Antiques
1906 Cherokee Street
St. Louis, MO 63118
314-771-5121
*Old books, china, silver plate,
crystal, old prints, lace. By
appointment only.*

Memories & Wishes Antiques
307 Marshall Street
Jefferson City, MO 65101
314-635-8944
*Furniture, glassware, clocks, mirrors,
pictures*

MONTANA

Jerome House Antiques
1721 Highland Street
Helena, MT 59601
406-442-1776
Furniture, documents, fine china, glass, primitives, clocks. By appointment only.

NEBRASKA

Antique Haven
1723 Vinton Street
Omaha, NE 68108
402-341-8661
Collectibles. By appointment only.

Flea Market Emporium
3235 South 13th Street
Lincoln, NE 68502
402-423-5380
Basic antiques and collectibles.

I Remember Antiques
6571 Maple Street
Omaha, NE 68104
402-556-6061
Collectibles, including Fiestaware, Red Wing, kitchen items from the 1930s and 1940s

NEVADA

Frontier Antique Mall
221 South Curry Street
Carson City, NV 89721
702-887-1466
Antiques and collectibles of all kinds

Granny's Nook & Cranny
Gypsy Caravan Mall
Las Vegas, NV 89104
702-598-1983
Victorian and mahogany furniture, Hummels, Royal Daltons, jewelry

Old West Antiques
111 Rice Street
Carson City, NV 89706
702-882-4650
Western antiques, glassware, silver, china, paintings

NEW HAMPSHIRE

Bert Savage Larch Lodge
Route 26
Center Strafford, NH 03815
603-269-7411
Antique rustic furniture and accessories, antique canoes. By appointment only.

NEW JERSEY

Americana by the Seashore
604 Broadway
Barnegat Light, NJ 08006
609-494-0656
19th-century oyster plates, antique cupboards, glassware, quilts, pillows, pictures

Greenwood Antiques
1918 Greenwood Avenue
Trenton, NJ 08609
609-586-6887
American and European paintings.
By appointment only.

King Charles Ltd.
48 Coryell Street
Lambertville, NJ 08530
609-397-9733
18th- and 19th-century English
and Continental furniture and
accessories

NEW MEXICO

Antique & Almost
1433 San Mateo Boulevard NE
Albuquerque, NM 87110
505-256-3600
Furniture, jewelry, Depression glass,
flatware, silver plate, sterling silver.
By appointment only.

Pegasus Antiques & Collectibles
1372 Cerrillos Road
Santa Fe, NM 87505
505-982-3333
Southwestern antiques

Roma Antiques
3904 Central Avenue SE
Albuquerque, NM 87108
505-266-6453
Prints, pin-ups, articles, primitives,
Roseville pottery

Gloria List
223 North Guadalupe #231
Santa Fe, NM 87505
505-988-4002
Southwest religious art and artifacts

NEW YORK

ABC Carpet & Home
888 Broadway
New York, NY 10003
212-473-3000
Antique furniture, accessories, rugs

America Hurrah
766 Madison Avenue
New York, NY 10021
212-635-1930
Antiques, quilts, American folk art,
Native American art

Casa El Patio
38 Newtown Lane
Easthampton, NY 11937
516-329-0300
McCoy pottery, candles, antique
painted furniture, accessories

Distant Origin
153 Mercer Street
New York, NY 10012
212-491-0024
Rustic antiques

Hope & Wilder Home
454 Broome Street
New York, NY 10013
212-966-9010
*Antique cupboards, accessories,
vintage and new fabrics*

Ruby Beets Antiques
Poxybogue Road & 27
Bridgehampton, NY 14873
516-537-2802

Susan P. Meisel Decorative Arts
133 Prince Street
New York, NY 10012
212-254-0137
*Collectibles, sailboats, Clarice Cliff
pottery, original pin-up art*

NORTH CAROLINA
Carolina Collectibles
11717 Six Forks Road
Raleigh, NC 27614
919-848-3778
*1920s-1930s furniture. By appoint-
ment only.*

Westmoore Pottery
4622 Busbee Road
Seagrove, NC 27341
910-464-3700
*Handmade and hand-decorated salt-
glazed stoneware in 17th- to 19th-
century styling*

NORTH DAKOTA
Le Fabeargé Antique Mall
200 West Main Avenue
Bismarck, ND 58501
701-221-2594
*Glassware, French enamelware,
1850s to 1960s furniture*

Wizard of Odds 'N Ends
1523 East Thayer Avenue
Bismarck, ND 58501
701-222-4175
Antique accessories

OHIO
Antiques Etcetera Mall
3265 North High Street
Columbus, OH 43202
614-447-2242
*Primitive furniture, pottery, South-
western jewelry*

Susie & Rich Burmann
118 South Barron Street
Eaton, OH 45320
513-456-1669
*American 18th- and 19th-century
furniture and accessories. By
appointment only.*

M. Dallas
P.O. Box 278
Danville, OH 43014
614-599-5919
*Flag plates, antique reproduction
spatterware*

Marjorie Stauffer
2244 Remsen Road
Medina, OH 44256
216-239-1443
*American 18th- and 19th-century
furniture and smalls in original
paints and finishes. By appointment only.*

Robert Zollinhofer
3845 Fenn Road
Medina, OH 44256
216-722-7544
*Pilgrim-century primitives. By
appointment only.*

OKLAHOMA
Apple Tree Antique Mall
1111 North Meridian Avenue
Oklahoma City, OK 73107
A variety of collectibles

Tomorrow Memories Antiques
411 Northwest 23rd Street
Oklahoma City, OK 73103
*1940s furniture, Depression glass-
ware, turn-of-the-century collectibles*

OREGON
The Bay Window
1312 Bay Street
Florence, OR 97439
503-997-2002
*Fine American and antique prints;
antiques, books, discoverables; custom picture framing*

Ellenburg Antiques &
  Collectibles
513 Highway 101
Florence, OR 97439
503-997-6430
*Buy and sell, estate sales, Depression
china, coins, carnival glassware*

Johnson House
216 Maple Street
Florence, OR 97439
503-997-8000
*Bed and breakfast located in the his-
toric waterfront district of Old Town*

Old Town Treasures
299 Maple Street
Florence, OR 97439
503-997-1364
*Antiques & collectibles; several
dealers under one roof; buy and sell
pre-1960 toys*

Molly Reed
30 N. Central
Medford, OR 97501
503-770-7103
Gifts and home accessories

Stars & Splendid Antique Mall
7027 S.E. Milwaukee Avenue
Portland, OR 97212
503-235-5990
*Portland's largest (30,000 square
feet) antique mall with 250 dealers*

The Withie's
5655 Suncreek Drive
Lake Oswego, OR 97035
503-620-0404
*Custom silk florals. By appoint-
ment only.*

PENNSYLVANIA

Lewis Keister Antiques
209 Market Street
Lewisburg, PA 17837
717-523-3945
Textiles, quilts, accessories

Period Furniture Designs
102 East Street Road
Kennett Square, PA 19348
610-444-6780
*18th- and 19th-century reproduction
furniture and folk art*

Judy Naftulin
7044 Ferry Road
New Hope, PA 18938
215-297-0702
*European and American furniture,
lighting, architectural elements,
garden ornaments, mirrors, frames,
textiles*

RHODE ISLAND

Cat's Pajamas
227 Wickenden Street
Providence, RI 02903
401-751-8440
20th-century antiques such as silver jewelry, Russel Wright pottery, glassware, chenille spreads

My Favorite Things
67 Weybossett Street
(The Arcade)
Providence, RI 02903
401-831-3332
Antique linens, lace, buttons, costume jewelry

SOUTH CAROLINA

Attic Fanatic Antique Malls
935 South Broad Street
Camden, SC 29020
803-787-9856
Period furniture, art glass, toys, Belleck porcelain

Heirloom Antiques &
  Collectibles
6000 Garners Ferry Road
Columbia, SC 29209
803-776-3955
Bric-a-brac, 18th-century furniture, antique jewelry

Thieves Market
502 Gadsden Street
Columbia, SC 29201
803-254-4997
Furniture, dinnerware, accessories

SOUTH DAKOTA

Antique & Furniture Mart
1112 West Main Street
Rapid City, SD 57701
605-341-3345
Turn-of-the-century oak furniture, collectibles, glassware, dishware

Gaslight Antiques
13490 Main Street
Rapid City, SD 57701
605-343-9276
1880s to 1950s furniture, glassware, jewelry

TENNESSEE

Antique Merchant's Mall
2015 8th Avenue South
Nashville, TN 37204
615-292-7811
Rare books, mahogany, walnut, and oak furniture, porcelain, china, crystal, sterling

Cane Ery Antique Mall
2207 21st Avenue South
Nashville, TN 37212
615-269-4780
American primitive and oak furniture, cane and basket repair and supplies

Joy Haley
102 Brighton Close
Nashville, TN 37205
615-297-6364
*High-end country painted furniture
and accessories*

TEXAS

American Higgledy Piggledy
302 East Main Street
Fredericksburg, TX 78624
210-997-8520
Linens, fabrics

Antique Pavilion
2311 Westheimer
Houston, TX 77098
713-520-9755
Quality antiques

True West
Rt. 3, Box 177-A
Goldwaite, TX 76844
915-648-2696
*Western, Santa Fe, American
country antiques*

UTAH

Pine Cupboard Antiques
247 East 300 South
Salt Lake City, UT 84111
801-359-6420
Pine furniture and Utah art

Salt Lake Antiques
279 East 300 South
Salt Lake City, UT 84111
801-322-1273
*Early English and American
antiques, Persian rugs, silver,
paintings*

VERMONT

The Clock Doctor, Inc.
South Street
Middletown Springs, VT 05143
802-235-2440
Antique mechanical clocks

Glad Rags Fine Vintage Antiques
6 State Street
Montpelier, VT 05602
802-223-1451
*Lamps, art pottery, postcards,
jewelry, glass, china, metal through
art deco period*

Sylvan Hill Antiques
Sylvan Road
Grafton, VT 05146
802-875-3954
*Period English and American
country furniture, specializing in
children's furniture. By appointment only.*

VIRGINIA

Baron's Antiques and
    Collectibles
1706 East Main Street
Richmond, VA 23223
804-643-0001
Eclectic

Hard Timz & Sunshine
244 London Bridge Center
Virginia Beach, VA 23454
804-463-7335
*Small furniture, glassware,
collectibles*

New Life Antiques & Keepsakes
6925 Lakeside Avenue
Richmond, VA 23228
804-264-9322
Primitive and Colonial furniture

WASHINGTON

Fircrest Country Store
612 Regents Boulevard
Fircrest, WA 98466
206-566-6886
Antiques, collectibles, gifts

Island Lady Antiques
55 Second Street
P.O. Box 3233
Friday Harbor, WA 98250
206-378-2890
American country antiques

WASHINGTON, DC

Antiques Anonymous
2627 Connecticut Avenue NW
Washington, DC 20008
202-332-5555
Eclectic, mostly jewelry

Cherishables
1608 20th Street NW
Washington, DC 20009
202-785-4087
*18th- and 19th-century American
furniture, quilts, and accessories*

Michael Getz Antiques
2918 M Street NW
Washington, DC 20007
202-338-3811
*Silver, fireplace equipment, lamps,
china*

WEST VIRGINIA

Smokey J Antics
600 Sissonville Drive
Sissonville, WV 25312
304-984-9783
*Dolls, old toys, trunks, rocking
chairs, clocks*

Split Rail Antiques
2580 Benson Drive
Charleston, WV 25302
304-342-6084
*Country antiques, early sporting
items. By appointment only.*

WISCONSIN

Antiques Mall of Madison
4748 Cottage Grove Road
Madison, WI 53716
608-222-2049
Eclectic

Larry's Used Furniture
2898 South Syene Road
Madison, WI 53711
608-271-8162
Doors, windows, furniture, rugs

Past Recollections
5735 South 27th Street
Greenfield, WI 53221
414-281-3099
*Primitive pieces, dishware, lamps,
rugs*

WYOMING

Old West Antiques & Cowboy
  Collectibles
1215 Sheridan Avenue
Cody, WY 82414
307-587-9014
Old West antiques and collectibles

Tomorrow's Treasures Antiques
903 East Lincolnway
Cheyenne, WY 82001
307-634-1900
*General line of antiques, glassware,
pottery*

Index

Italicized page numbers refer to photographs

Adamson, Jack, 172
Advertising boxes, *53*
Advertising figures, *80*
Airplanes made from Coke and Pepsi containers, *170*
Album covers, 172
American antiques, 16
Angelitos, 180
Anthony, Carol, 54–61
"Antiqued" finish, *53*
Antiques
    American antiques, 16
    caring for, 98
    defining characteristics, 17
    investment value, 25
    pricing of, 82
    shopping for, 150
Antiques Collecting (Blade), 11
Antiques shops, 150
Antiques shows and markets, 12, 150
Armoires, *89*
Arrangement techniques, *33*
Arts and Crafts-style beds, *164*
Artwork displays, *56, 57*, 68, *73, 86, 141, 158*
Auctions, 150

Bakelite products, 172
Ballrooms, *127*
Balls, cloth and leather, *152*
Banister-back chairs, *18, 142, 148*
Bars, *129*
Baskets, 44, *183*
    care for, 98
    lightship baskets, *25*
    Native American baskets, *113, 115*
Bathrooms, *51, 88, 191*
Becketts, *157*
Bed hangings, *43*
Bedrooms, *30–31, 43, 61, 80, 108, 122, 144, 148, 158, 191*
Beds, *67, 75, 190*
    Arts and Crafts-style beds, *164*
    Empire beds, *141*
    sassafras-log beds, *50*
    Sheraton youth beds, *128*
Bed spreads, *144*
Bent willow chairs, *165*
Bibelots, *67*
Birdcages, *30*
Birds-on-a-wire sculptures, *159*
Black walnut wood, 132
Blade, Timothy Trent, 11
Blakeslee, Burritt, 128
Blanket chests, *80, 107, 144, 153*
Blankets, *94*
    Third Phase Chief's blankets, *40*
    trade blankets, 44
Books-as-objects, 76, *79*
"Boonton" dishes, *171*
Bottlecap figures, 188

Bottle whimsies, *78*, 79, *79, 191*
Bowles, Skipper and Olga, 70–75
Bowls, *23, 85, 97, 161*
Boxes, *109*
    advertising boxes, *53*
    lattice boxes, *87*
    painted pantry boxes, *143*
Buffalo-hide paintings, *43*
Bultos, 180
Burden, Joe, *166*
Burmann, Susie and Richard, 12, 104–109
Burridge, Mildred, *121*

Cadillac Jack (McMurtry), 102
Candlestands, *24, 77*
Candlesticks, *36*
Caring for antiques, 98
Cash, Dianne and Berry, 36–43
Chairs
    banister-back chairs, *18, 142, 148*
    bent willow chairs, *165*
    ladderback chairs, *24*, 134, *146–147*
    Mexican country chairs, *58*
    North Carolina corner chairs, *71*
    Queen Anne maple chairs, *127*
    split-wood caned seat chairs, *78*
    upholstered pieces, *135*
    Windsor chairs, *122, 132, 156, 157*
Chess sets, *129*
Chests, *126*
    blanket chests, *80, 107, 144, 153*
    English oak chests, *141*
    sea chests, *115*
Chests of drawers, *117, 126, 145, 159*
Childhood mementos, *60*
Chimayo weavings, 44
China, Staffordshire, *28*
Christiansen, Sigrid, 81
Christmas decorating, 97, *97*
Cigar store figures, *130*
Clocks
    grandfather clocks, *131*
    Mickey Mouse alarm clocks, *130*
Codman, Ogden, Jr., 34
Collectibles, 17
Collectors, 10
    characteristics of, 10–11, 13
    dealer-collector relationship, 19, 23
Color schemes, 88, 89, *96*
Conrad, Judy and Dennis, 18–25, 150
Cookie cutters, *47*
Cooper, Mary and Marc, 84–89
Cote, Adrian, 112–117
"Courting" gifts, *168*
Cowboy artifacts, 172
Cowhide rugs, *64*
Cradles, *108, 148*
Creamware, *28*
Cristos, 180
Croquet balls, *140*
Cupboards, *23, 46, 53, 72, 74, 90, 122, 142, 157, 162–163, 188, 189*
Curtains, *25, 145*

Dancing toys, 77
Davis, Preacher Ben, *190*
Dealers, 10, 102–103
    characteristics of, 11–13
    dealer-collector relationship, 19, 23
    as educators, 12–13, 23
    pickers, 118
    profit requirements, 118
    specialization by, 12
    trading up, 142
Decoration of Houses, The (Wharton and Codman), 34
Demilune mahogany tables, *134*
Desks, *49*
Dining rooms, *88, 94, 97, 114, 124–125, 139, 149*
Doherty, Barbara, 68, 120–125
Dolls
    Kachina, 44
    nuthead and cloth, *190*
Dough tables, *79*
Dry sinks, *160, 162–163*, 165
Dust concerns, 98

Eames, Charles, *169*
Eastern white oak wood, 132
Eclectic collections, 68–69, *68, 69*
Eichhorn, Jacqueline and Douglas, 166–171, 172
Empire beds, *141*
Enamelware, 172
English oak chests, *141*
Estate sales, 150
Ex votos, 180

Finials, *178*
Flea markets, 150
Floor cloths, *24*
Floor paintings, *104, 105, 158, 184*
Found collections, 26, *26, 27*
Foyers, *37, 76*
Freund, Thatcher, 10
Future of collecting, 172

Gas pumps, *73*
Gates, *58*
"General store" atmosphere, *155*
George, Judith, 112–117
Gephart, Barbara, *109*
Glasser, Carol and Mark, 28–33
Globes, world, 172
Glover, Joseph, *79*
Grandfather clocks, *131*
Great Camp furniture, 38

Haley, Joy and Bob, 134–141
Harrison Home, 8–10
Hearths, *122, 130*
Heat and humidity concerns, 98
Hewell, Grace Nell, *169*
Hickory wood, 132, *184*
Hooked rugs, *130, 156*
Horses, painted folk-art, *122*
House restorations, 107, *107*, 109, 128

Hunt boards, *114*
Hutch tables, *145*

Icons, *63*
Idlewild, 137, *139*
Investment value of antiques, 25
Ironwork, *116*

Kachina dolls, 44
Keeping rooms, *146–147*, 157
King, Isaac, 145
Kitchens, *20–21*, 72, *96*, *137*, *171*, *178*,
    188

Ladderback chairs, *24*, 134, *146–147*
Lattice boxes, *87*
Laundry hampers, *159*
Lauren, Ralph, 118
Lazy Susan tables, *139*
Letter-writing, 51
Levey, Richard, 76–81
Libraries, *32*
Lich, Rod, 12, 82, 182–191
Light concerns, 98
Lightship baskets, *25*
Limestone whimsies, *185*
List, Gloria, 12, 69, 82, 174–179, 180
Living rooms, *29*, *59*, *65*, *74*, *87*, *92–93*,
    136, *154*, *184*
Log cabins, *50*, 70, *70–75*, *73*, *75*
Loving cup trophies, 172

MacDonald, Elizabeth, *59*, 61
Mantel decorations, 25
Mantels, *52*
Maps, *185*
Marsden, Doug, *38*
Marston House, 154, *155*
McAdams family, *183*, 187
McCormick, Mark and Lisa, 160–165
McMurtry, Larry, 102
Mexican country chairs, *58*
Mickey Mouse alarm clocks, *130*
Midcentury Americana, *169*, *171*, 172
Milagros, *39*, *178*
Miniature houses, *52*, *160*, *164*, *168*
Mirrors, *134*
Mooseskins, *95*
Mrozinski, Sharon and Paul, 152–159
Mugs, *129*
Murals, *19*, *121*

Native American clothing, *42–43*
Native American crafts, 44, *44*, *45*, *113*,
    114, *115*, 117, *117*
Natural objects, 26, *26*, *27*
Navajo rugs, 44, *113*
Nichos, 180
Nonesuch Gallery, 176
North Carolina corner chairs, *71*
Nuthead and cloth dolls, *190*

Objects of Desire (Freund), 10
Optiques, *87*
Oushak rugs, *32*

Painted furniture, 79, 110, *110*, *111*
Paint-finishing, *46*
Pantry boxes, *143*
Papier-mâché animals, *153*, *157*

Parrett, Susan, 182–191
Patio furniture, *164*
Peattie, Donald Culross, 132
Pedestal sinks, *141*
Pianos, *40*
Pickers, 118
Picture frames, *63*, *64*, *66*, 68, *184*
Pineapple Primitives, 120
Plates, *23*
Plympton House, *145*
Polizzi, Tasha and Jack, 90–97
Porter, Rufus, *19*
Pot hooks, *186–187*
Pottery, *40*, 44, *76*, *84*, 89, *109*
Pricing of antiques, 82
Prison art, *167*

Queen Anne maple chairs, *127*
Quilts, *75*, *80*, 172, 174, 176, 184, *184*

Ranges, *171*
Redware crock canisters, *21*
Reed, Melinda, 61
Religious art and artifacts, 12–13, *58*, *63*,
    174, *175*, *176–180*, *176*, *177*, *178*,
    179, *180*, *181*
Reredos, 180
Retablos, 180
Rifles, *74*, *130*
Rocking horses, *125*, *140*
Rugs, *80*
    cowhide rugs, *64*
    hooked rugs, *130*, *156*
    Navajo rugs, 44, *113*
    Oushak rugs, *32*

Saltillo weavings, *97*
Santeros, 180
Santero village art, 180
Santos, *38*, 180
Sassafras-log beds, *50*
Sawbuck tables, *159*
Scandinavian tables, *76*
Schoolgirl art, 172
Scrub-top tables, *138*, *146–147*
Sea chests, *115*
Sea-motif decorations, 25
Seashore, objects found at, 26
Secretaries, *136*
Settles, *71*, *147*
'70s artifacts, 172
Shawls, *29*
Sheraton youth beds, *128*
Shoefoot hutch tables, *127*
Shopping for antiques, 150
Shutters, *51*
    with cutout motifs, 172
Signs, old, *154*
Silhouettes, *88*
Silver, care for, 98
Sinks
    dry sinks, *160*, *162–163*, 165
    pedestal sinks, *141*
Smalls, 34, *34*, *35*
Smoking paraphernalia, 172
Sofas, *87*
Southard, Charlie, 57
Split-wood caned seat chairs, *78*
Sporting folk art, 172
Stearns, Hannah and Art, 46–53

Stencilling, *106*, 109
Stepstools, *182*
Stoneware, *143*
Sugar containers, *145*
Sugar maple wood, 132
Sunrooms, *71*
Swann, Larry, *58*, 61

Tables, *20–21*, *162–163*
    demilune mahogany tables, *134*
    dough tables, *79*
    hutch tables, *145*
    lazy Susan tables, *139*
    sawbuck tables, *159*
    Scandinavian tables, *76*
    scrub-top tables, *138*, *146–147*
    shoefoot hutch tables, *127*
    tea tables, *123*, *148*
    writing tables, *30*
Tableware, hotel silver, 172
Tea tables, *123*, *148*
Technology, concealment of, *48*, *62*
Teddy bears, *153*
Textiles, care for, 98
Third Phase Chief's blankets, *40*
Tin crafts, *40–41*, 180
Toby mugs, *129*
Toilet-paper dispensers, 89
Tole trays, *32*
Topiaries, *122*
Totem poles, *165*
T. P. Saddleblanket & Trading, Inc., 94
Trade blankets, 44
Tramp art, *184*, 188
Travel souvenirs, 172
Treen jars, *76*
Trophies, *74*, 172
Trunks, *155*

Upholstered pieces, *135*
Urns, *29*, *157*
Utopian-society furniture, 81

Ventriloquist's dummies, *170*

Wall-on-wheels, *58*
Wallpaper, *129*
Wardrobes, *140*
Weathervanes, *112*, *116*, 166
Webb, Margaret, *58*
West, Jerry, 57
Wharton, Edith, 34
Wheat, Joe Ben, 114
White ash wood, 132
White pine wood, 132
Wigstands, *127*
Wild black cherry wood, 132
Wilderness areas, objects found in, 26
Williams, Dottie, 19, 23
Windham, Ellen, 34, 62–67, 68, 69
Windsor chairs, *122*, *132*, *156*, *157*
Wire household products, 172
Wood
    care for, 98
    types of, 132
Woods, objects found in, 26
Wool skeins, *22*
Writing tables, *30*

Zollinhofer, Robert, 118, 126–131